DEAR Jack + Pat
Hope you ENJOy the
book - It was a
pleasure to write

Yellow Jacket
Football
in Hard Times and Good

Raymond J. Golarz

authorHOUSE®

AuthorHouse™
1663 Liberty Drive
Bloomington, IN 47403
www.authorhouse.com
Phone: 1-800-839-8640

First published by AuthorHouse 6/23/2010

ISBN: 978-1-4520-2574-2 (e)
ISBN: 978-1-4520-2573-5 (sc)

Library of Congress Control Number: 2010907644

Printed in the United States of America
Bloomington, Indiana

This book is printed on acid-free paper.

TO THE TEENAGE CHILDREN OF POLAND

WHO HAD THE COURAGE TO LEAVE THEIR

HOMES AND TRAVEL TO A NEW LAND

FOR THE BENEFIT

OF THEIR YET UNBORN

CHILDREN

AND THEIR POSTERITY

Table of Contents

Acknowledgments

To my Aunt Rose Koral, for otherwise who could have remembered Zothkiewicz's grocery store on Kenwood Street and so many other authentic details that make this book so special.

To my wife Marion whose creativity is responsible for so much of the book, including the design, concept, and arrangement of the cover, the title selection, so many of the chapter titles, the writing of the introduction, the text for the back cover and her unending and sympathetic guidance to an author trying to say it just the right way. Most of our best arguments I lost.

To my cousin Tony Koral who was always there for my phone calls. Calls that often had an unanswerable question or a creative idea that needed a quick death or calls that just needed his patient ear to allow this author to talk it through.

To my daughter Tanya Scherschel, herself a gifted writer, and her husband John for so many hours of technical assistance from the beginning of this endeavor to the end.

To my cousin Anita Galosich for information regarding her dad, Walt Golarz as it related to the time period of this book.

To Buddy Borbely, son of Kal Borbely, for use of the "Yellow Jacket 35" emblem that belonged to his father and for conversations as well as for an old newspaper article that identified some Yellow Jacket players Lefty could not remember.

And finally, to Mark Wusic, son of Mike Wusic, for the rare team picture of the Yellow Jackets taken in the location of their home field with Pullman Standard in the background, and Steve Euvino, editor of the Northwest Indiana Catholic for the pictures of Old Saint Mary's Church and picture of the St. Mary's sisters.

Introduction

There are many ways to write a story about a set of events or an era which occurred in the past. You can consult written records. You can visit or revisit these places. You can probe your memories and the memories of others. Or if you have lived, breathed and pondered this era long and hard enough, you can develop an intuitive sense that will allow you to fill in the empty spaces left by incomplete written records or faded memories- empty spaces not unlike incomplete DNA strands. This capacity to fill in will thus allow you to recreate the essence of how people acted, how they spoke, what they hoped for, and how they inhaled and exhaled life even though you were never there.

This is exactly what Raymond Golarz has done with *Yellow Jacket Football in Hard Times and Good*, so that the Twenty First Century reader of his book about the residents of this East Hammond community may better understand their lives. He has reached back into his life and the lives of so many others to tell this compelling story. Using keen insight and drawing upon a wealth of personal knowledge and information gained from the few remaining living witnesses, he completely immerses the reader in this Polish community during the Depression years of the mid-thirties. Adding to these sources, the author was able to confirm much of the material and information contained in this book by spending extensive hours researching newspaper archives and other documents. In addition he examined such items as the Polish books his grandfather brought to America, birth certificates, dance ticket stubs, pictures, ethnic clothing, old written records, audio tapes, awards and a plethora of artifacts and memorabilia he has collected all of his life.

One of the most cherished sources was, of course, his own father Lefty Golarz, a primary source in his first book on this topic. Much of what is related about the Yellow Jackets, their players and their games, came directly from Lefty. But, as often happens for researchers in the course of digging deeper, Golarz found parallel stories developing.

Here, along with the story of the Yellow Jacket football team, came the stories of both other semi-pro teams and an emerging national professional football league with its heavily documented bounces and bumps along an uncharted and untested new road.

This would be enough for any fan of football, but this jewel of Americana is richly embedded in another piece of the American mosaic—the massive migration of those who came from Poland in the Nineteenth and early Twentieth Centuries. These immigrants and their children are the people who come so vibrantly alive in the pages of this new book—*Yellow Jacket Football In Hard Times And Good*.

Again, as with *When the Yellow Jackets Played*, we are transported to and through exciting, demanding football games and again we meet the players we became familiar with and meet many new ones as well. But, what is true for *When the Yellow Jackets Played* (the snapshot of the 1936 Polish ghetto) is even truer for this new book (a snapshot of the 1934 and 1935 years) as East Hammond suffered the deepest depths of the Depression. This time we get to know in much more detail the struggles and challenges the Depression brought to health and hearth, and we get to know how faith, good will, hard work, charity, tradition and sacrifice helped this community do more than simply survive. We share in the joys and appreciation that comes from not only a hard fought victory, but from a half cup of coffee around a pot bellied stove after a middle of the night trek along the railroad tracks—a trek taken to collect the coal that was the generous gift of engineers who shook it loose from their trains. We enter into the Golarz home to join in the festivities of a traditional Christmas meal, carefully saved for. We get a chance to dance and play and, yes, hoist a few, to raise money for a family devastated by the tragic injury of its only breadwinner. Along with Lefty we hitch a ride on a boxcar of one of the giant steam engines of that day. We take a journey to faraway New York City, and meet along the way some World War I veterans on their way to Washington D.C., some lost souls, some very kind souls, and some very mean ones, as well.

Whether you are turning pages to discover how the games come out, see if the lost purse with its treasured Christmas money is found, or if the Yellow Jackets will find enough coal to stoke their families' furnaces, you will come closer to knowing and enjoying this immigration story not known very well by many, even today.

You know, we often hear people say, "We are a nation of immigrants," but sometimes the import of that statement gets lost, for we forget, if we ever really understood, the story of how their lives intertwined with and enhanced the life of our country. Ray Golarz, does remember, does understand, and with his unique story-telling he teaches us and reminds us of what it means to say, "We are a nation of immigrants." In so doing he makes it clear that the story of immigrant lives is still one of the most profound stories of this great democracy.

Note to the reader:

The author has chosen to categorize this account as a work of creative non-fiction. He has done so because he used detailed and verifiable facts culled from his research of newspaper accounts and other historical sources as well as his own memory and life experiences. In addition, he has drawn upon the memories of the very few persons still living and lucid who can reconstruct a portion of these times, and, of course, the wealth of information given to him by Lefty. Even with all of this authentic detail, however, he still needed to rely upon the understanding he gained while being immersed in this culture from the time he was very young until he was an adult. His understanding has allowed him to go beyond facts and create portraits of the many people and friends who appear in these pages.

I would also like to call attention to a special aspect of this story. Because of the author's many years of having lived with first generation immigrants, he gained the ability to authentically recreate their attempt at the English language. This attempt is often referred to as "broken English." For the author it was a unique and treasured way of speaking. In several sections of the book, he uses his proficiency in this regard and shares with the reader what this attempt at the English language would sound like. So, where his characters do put aside their mother tongue, he has come very close to portraying the unique idiom and syntax of that particular kind of broken English, a broken English spoken to him often as the elders of his culture attempted to, "say it in the English."

In order to maintain his intent to convey this way of communicating, he has developed a phonetic transcription to transcribe such dialogue. However, this is a difficult task and there is no easy way to completely replicate the sounds. Moreover, it is even more difficult to convey the rhythm in which the individual syllables of English words often are heavily accented and haltingly connected. But, there are some consistencies which may be helpful to the reader. For example, "w" is pronounced like the English "v" and as is the case with most non-native speakers, prepositions are often dropped and the verb forms of "to be" are often omitted, altered, or appear in a different order.

Finally, it should be apparent that in some instances it was necessary for the author to take some license with representations of conversations, experiences or events. Thus, as is common to the fiction genre, some of this story is the result of using facts and weaving them with the author's interpretation and presentation of what would have logically and typically been an authentic occurrence.

Throughout this telling, despite the distance of time and place, the people who come alive in these stories, I am sure, were never far away. I like to think that it is really their voices that are poured out onto these pages because they still reside in the spirit of their latest and, I think, their best story-teller.

Marion Golarz

Being Hungry

John "Heinie" Milobar and "Johnny Five" Gorski had gotten to Wusic's gas station early that morning. The night before, they had promised old man Wusic that they would come by and clean up before he got there to open the station at 6:00 am. They got right to it, Johnny putting away chairs from a late Yellow Jacket team meeting the night before and Heinie busily sweeping around the gas pumps and entrance to the gas station with an old broom that had seen its better days some years ago. "Hey Heinie, How many games did 'Wolf' (Walter Golarz) say we had left this season?"

"Two, I think, next week away against Calumet City and then two weeks later here at home against Chicago Heights."

"Well, as banged up as everyone is that will make two tough games."

Heinie agreed, "You got it."

"Hey Heinie, what's that you just uncovered in the grease with your broom? Here let me get it."

"Nah, I'll get it, I'm sweepin.'"

"Well, what is it?"

Heinie said quietly while he rubbed off the grease, "It's a nickel."

"No shit, here give it to me."

"No, I picked it up."

"Yeah, but I saw it first."

Heinie, "Let's just say it's ours."

"Bullshit."

"Look, Johnny, I don't want to fight you for a nickel, but I will."

"OK, OK, it's ours. Well, what do you want to do with it?"

Heinie answered, "Well let's finish up and when old man Wusic gets here we'll go to the OK Bakery for a roll or a donut."

Within 15 minutes Mr. Wusic had arrived and Heinie and Johnny were taking a short, quick walk to the OK Bakery. Down Colombia Avenue to Ames Street, left on Ames, down one block to the bakery.

"Hey, Heinie, what do you want to get?"

"A chocolate donut, they're easy to split and I love chocolate."

"Yeah, but it has a hole in the middle. Think of all you don't get when you buy a donut with a hole in the middle –all that empty space, and anyway I'm not that excited about chocolate."

Heinie asks, "Well, what do you think?"

"Get some kind of roll filled with something like prune or raspberry or…"

"OK, raspberry it is, but remember they're harder to break in half."

"I know –we'll do it slow. We'll do it slow."

At this point they were 50 or so yards from the bakery, but already they could smell the aromas of fresh baked breads and pastries. The speed of their salivation would have put Pavlov's dogs to shame. Finally, they reached the side door to the bakery – the doorway used by those living in the community. They opened the door and were greeted by aromas that were now overpowering.

Toward the back of the bakery were two large ovens where bakers were moving breads in and out with gigantic flat wooden paddles. Smaller ovens were being used to prepare other baked goods. To the left they spotted fresh trays of donuts and rolls being taken to the front of the bakery where

3

most selling and purchasing took place. Much was sold to companies and municipalities in a six to seven mile area surrounding the bakery. Lever Brothers Soap Factory each morning had someone pick up five dozen rolls and two loaves of bread, the Hammond City Hall four dozen rolls, etc.

Heinie and Johnny's purchase that morning would be less substantial. They passed over the five cents, and then with the fresh raspberry filled roll in hand, they were out the side door of the bakery and sat down on a nearby curb. Now, carefully, they broke the roll in half. This was accomplished to both of their surgical satisfactions. Each holding their share of the roll, they continued to enjoy the aroma. Finally, in silence they slowly, very slowly, ate their portion of the roll–each saving a bit of filling for the last bite. They continued to sit there for a long moment, licking fingers for a taste of a roll that was no longer there. Finally, Johnny, without looking up from his hands, said "Heinie?"

"Yeah?"

"I don't remember being this poor and hungry when we were kids."

Heinie simply shook his head and without looking up responded, "We weren't, Johnny, we weren't."

They then sat there for a long time. The experience of the taste of the roll they would remember and treasure, but they would remember for an even longer time that they were still hungry–very hungry.

Heinie from Lefty's
1937 Wedding Party Photo

A Community of Farmers

East Hammond wasn't a big community. Columbia Avenue on the east and the Yellow Jacket football field and Pullman Standard east of that. On the west was the brickyard, many railroad tracks, and two separate coal yards. Immediately beyond that was Calumet Avenue. South was the incinerator, railroad tracks and the ice company. North was Conkey Street with homes filling most of the 900 Block. The 1000 and 1100 blocks of Conkey made up what East Hammond relied upon for most of its shopping: a drug store, poultry house, two candy stores, two theaters, a clothing store, milk shop, barber shop, Brooks House of Christian Services and a church serving the black community. Scattered throughout the neighborhood were many corner grocery stores, a good number of bars, the OK Bakery and Trinity

Hall. St. Mary's Catholic Church and grade school were three blocks north of Conkey. A full 90% of those who attended St. Mary's lived in East Hammond.

Virtually every lot or extended lot in East Hammond had been built on. Many of the individual properties were more than a single lot. They were a lot and a half or two lots. The standard lots had a 60 foot frontage and went back about 130 feet where the lots met the alleyway. The properties that were a lot and a half had a 90 foot frontage and the two lot properties had a frontage of 120 feet. The alleyways ran throughout the neighborhood, were about 12 feet wide and were gravel.

Most of the residents of the East Hammond community were born in foreign lands, primarily Poland. For the most part, their children were born in the United States. Polish and other foreign tongues were spoken in the homes. Children grew up bilingual. Their fathers had a better command of English than their mothers since fathers worked outside of the home in jobs that required verbal interaction. St. Mary's grade school had nuns who came from Poland. And both English and Polish were part of the standard curriculum.

Before leaving Poland to come to the United States, most of the East Hammond residents had lived in rural farming communities. Most of these East Hammond residents came specifically from the southeast corner of Poland, an area known as Galicia. This area had many mountains and forests, but also contained much farm land with many small farming communities. Over the years, this territory was controlled by Poland, sometimes Russia, and also sometimes Austria. During the great Polish migration to the United States in the early Twentieth Century, many Poles were surprised and distraught to find that their birth certificates actually declared them to be Austrian, but they were in their hearts, Polish.

Further, they were not just Polish, they were proud Polish, and they were Polish farmers. Thus, as they purchased lots upon which to build their homes, they often purchased one and a half lots or two lots so that they could plant extensive food gardens and fruit trees both behind and on the side of their homes. They would also often have poultry and cages for such near the backs of their property near the alleyways. They were skilled at growing and canning what they grew – essential skills for a depression community in the mid 1930's.

Like so many of these new American farmers, Ma Golarz had planted a lot of string beans this year. And the harvest was good. So, Andy and Anne, the kid brother and sister of Lefty and Walt, would spend all morning picking and snapping in the back of the yard. They had a couple of old boxes to sit on and several large buckets for the beans. Ma was already in the kitchen sterilizing a couple dozen quart jars. By season's end, she would can string beans, tomatoes, beets, corn, carrots, and dill pickles from cucumbers.

Andy and Anne enjoyed the preparation done with the cucumbers. Most of the East Hammond residents had their own large steel wash tub, some thirty inches in diameter, and about twelve inches deep. It was commonly referred to as the "balia," Polish for wash tub. On the day cucumbers were picked, the balia would be filled with water. Then the cucumbers would be thrown in. There they would be scrubbed gently with brushes and then put into clean water. From the clean water, they would be placed into a large, stainless steel pan containing a mixture of water, vinegar, pickling salt and sugar. This would be brought to a boil. From there they would be placed into canning jars with dill that had also been grown in the garden.

10

Finally, Ma would add dill seeds and a hot vinegar mixture. All of this--the amount of vinegar, dill, and seeds- would be done, keeping in mind the specific taste preferences of Pa and her family.

Pa was a carpenter, as were many of the men of East Hammond who worked at Pullman Standard and surrounding construction companies. On their jobs at Pullman they built boxcars. Their skills they brought back to their homes and to their community. When any construction in the community was done, such as the building of a house, adding a porch to an existing house, a garage, or even a large shed, there would be ample workmen in the form of friends and neighbors. This meant that when the job was big enough, sons were brought to do the less skilled jobs and be mentored in the skilled work. Thus, Walt, Lefty, Kal, Alex, Pulkowski, Chester, and many other Yellow Jackets and their neighborhood friends became quite adept at a full range of construction skills by the time they were young adults. Interestingly, some of the skilled tasks their fathers introduced them to were not simply mainstream, but rather adjunct and caught them off guard as Lefty and Walt relayed when they told the story about the time their father decided to make a stone grinding wheel:

"We're gonna make a what?" Lefty said to Walt.

"A stone grinding wheel to sharpen tools and knives."

"Walt, where the hell did Pa get that idea?"

"Don't know, Left, but he's buyin' the block of stone tomorrow."

"Block! Block! A block sounds square, Walt. How the hell do we get from square to round?"

"Sounds fun, doesn't it, Left?"

"I can just see me, Walt, sanding down a stone for six hours with a huge file, then going out and trying to throw a football with a rubber arm."

"Learn to throw with the other arm, Left."

"Aw, shit!"

"Ah, c'mon, Left, think of it this way. If we do a good enough job, old man Wusic might hire us to make four stone wheels to replace the tires on his truck."

"Walt, this is no time to joke around. Today, when I woke up, if you had told me, that my future involved making a round stone grinding wheel out of a square stone block, well, well….aw, shit!"

Walt and Lefty, of course, completed their task, and Pa fixed a mechanism whereby they could rotate the wheel. They mounted it and added it to their collection of tools, a collection that had been occasionally purchased, sometimes traded for, and most often, made, a collection that they learned to care for and learned to repair. A collection that they over the years took pride in, and eventually passed down to their sons along with stories that surrounded how the tool came to be. Stories that to them were as much a gift as the tool itself.

Pa's Tools and Toolchest

Yellow Jackets Don't Ask
Each Other to Play Hurt

Wusic's gas station was situated on the west side of Columbia Avenue between Moss and Kenwood Streets. It was the only gas station in East Hammond. If the Yellow Jacket football team had a place they could call their own, or if they had a locker room of any kind, it would have been the addition to Wusic's built around 1931 by those players of the 1931 team. They more than likely used for its construction, lumber from the many wood piles that dotted back yards throughout the East Hammond neighborhood.

The station itself was actually fairly big with two Shell gas pumps outside. There was a general main room with a large picture window. The cash register rested on a glass case with a portion of the glass cracked and taped. Small items like patches for inner tubes, grease, grease guns, hoses of various types and lengths were on display on boxes and on the wall. In addition, a large clock was centered on the wall opposite the wall displaying the hoses. Next to the clock was an old, fading Coca-Cola sign. This room opened into a large garage area with its hydraulic lift for cars and its large door that opened upwards to allow sufficient space to move cars and or trucks in and out. Along side of this garage area was the addition known as the Yellow Jacket Room. Entrance to this room was a simple doorway from the garage area of the gas station. The room itself was no more than 10 feet by 11 feet. It had a large five-by-seven foot window that looked onto Columbia Avenue. In the back corner of the room was a small pot-bellied iron stove that vented through the ceiling and warmed the area very well in winter months. The room also had some old chairs and a very old but quite stable dark red table. The wall in the back of this room opposite the window had been painted black by the Yellow Jackets and served as an adequate chalkboard to diagram plays when their meetings were held for such purposes.

Walt Golarz , nicknamed "Wolf," the unofficial yet recognized team captain, said to "Fatty" Grisha, "Is everyone here yet?"

Fatty, former fullback on the very successful 1921-1925 Hammond Boosters semi-pro team replied, "Just a few more Wolf, looks like Heinie, Topolski and Stoming aren't here yet."

"Well, let me know when they all get in and we'll start the meeting."

It was Thursday at 4:00 p.m. and the Yellow Jacket team was meeting at Wusic's. This coming Sunday at 2:00 p.m. would be an away game at Calumet City, Illinois. Hammond actually bordered Calumet City and their border was the Indiana- Illinois state line, thus not a game very far away, but far enough, and an intense rivalry. Walt said, "OK, guys quiet down a little. "Fatty, Lefty? Is everyone here?"

Lefty, Walt's younger brother replied, "Only one not here Walt is George Stoming. Remember he told all of us a couple of days ago that he wouldn't be able to make it because he had to help his pa."

"Thanks Left. I remember. OK, guys I know it's a little tight in here but try to make yourselves comfortable. Now I want to turn it over to Fatty. He has to talk to us about injuries and the upcoming game with Cal City. Some of you won't like to hear what he has to say, but listen anyway. What he has to say is what we believe is in your best interest and our best interest as a team."

Fatty took over, "Men, you know who we are playin' this Sunday. Cal City. They are hands down the meanest bunch of football players we will face all season. If you look like you're limping they'll go after it. If you're favoring one arm and not playing as well with the other, they'll notice it and go after it. If they can hurt ya, they will. If they can knock ya out of the game or season, they will. For many of you I'm not telling ya anything new, you've played 'em before. Am I telling ya you're not as tough as they are? Hell no. We're as tough, if not tougher than any team we play. We just don't play that way."

Three weeks ago we were playin' Crown Point, remember?"

Walt motions to Fatty to stop the story, but Fatty looks at Walt and says, "Let me tell 'em, they need to hear it."

Walt dropped his head and Fatty continued.

"They had a young, inexperienced, shifty little linebacker. Remember, just full of piss and vinegar. Well, by the second quarter he was gettin' slower.

Walt, comin' through the line had hit him full-on two or three times, and then, Lefty, remember you hit him full-on too." Lefty nodded. Fatty continued.

"Well, then Walt came through one more time. The kid didn't even try to wrap, just stood his ground there and took the hit. After the play, Walt stood over the kid, offered the kid his hand for the kid to get up and the kid couldn't raise his arm, couldn't raise it even though he tried. Then, Walt called a time out and went to their captain. They talked while we all stood there wondering what the hell was going on . Then their captain took the kid off of the field. He had to guide the kid to their bench. After the game, remember their captain trying to find Walt as we were getting into Wusic's truck? The captain told Walt how much their team appreciated what we did. The kid still couldn't tell them where he was. By the way, that little piss and vinegar linebacker was the captain's kid brother. We have heard since that he left the game that day with a severe concussion and a dislocated right shoulder."

Fatty paused for a long time. It was quiet in the room. Then in a quieter voice Fatty continued.

"We have some guys who need to come off of the field. You won't play against Cal City and a few of ya may not make the Chicago Heights game. Johnny Topolski, you got knocked out in the game before our last game, and in our last game you had a concussion. You need to sit out this game and probably Chicago Heights too."

Johnny resisted. "Hey Fats. I'm fine, feel great, can run like a deer."

"Johnny it doesn't have anything to do with how fast ya are. Wolf and I even checked with "Huffy" (Carl Huffine, coach of Hammond High) and Johnny Long (revered East Hammond community boxing coach). Both of 'em said the most serious injury is a head injury, and you never mess around with a head injury. Sorry, Johnny."

Johnny somewhat muffled, "Aw, shit."

"Mike Juscik."

Juscik replied, "Yeah, Fats, I know."

"How bad is it today, Mike," asked Fatty.

Mike explained, "Well this morning not bad. Then I said, 'piss on it. I'm gonna walk on it—the hell with the pain. So, I walked all the way from my house , y'know, about five blocks."

Fatty said, "and..."

"Hurts like hell."

20

"Which knee is it again, Mike?"

"The left one."

"Can you touch it?"

"Wouldn't really want to."

"Would ya mind if we look at it, Mike?"

"Nah."

Fatty turned to several team members, "Some of you guys help Mike drop his pants gently so that we can see his knee." Upon seeing the knee, Fatty says, "Damn, Mike, it's almost 1 ½ times the size of your right one."

"Kind of swelled, huh."

Wolf moved in and looked at the knee, then said to Mike, "Mike y'know you're gonna have to stay off of this, or it will never get better."

"I know, Wolf, I know."

Wolf told the guys to help him get his pants back on, and then he says to Wusic, "Can you drive Mike home in the truck and on the way past my house pick up a pair of crutches in my basement. Lefty needed them a few years ago during high school. That okay with you, Left?"

Lefty nodded and replied, "Kal (Borbely) and I will go with Mike, get the crutches, and show Mike how to adjust 'em."

Walt replied, "Thanks, Left."

Walt looked at Fatty and says "Go ahead, Fatty."

Fatty looked at the team and said, "Tony Hayduk,"

Tony responded, "Yeah."

"How are the ribs?"

Tony says, "Broken."

"How many, Tony?"

"The doc said two."

"Well, Tony, you understand…"

Tony cut him off and appealed, "Look Fatty, I know they're broken but me and some of the guys just read in the paper that Jeboski on the Chicago Bears has two broken ribs and they're going to tape him up an' he's gonna play their next game. If I get taped, I know I can do it."

"Look Tony, no question that taping is an option, but we all know it's a dangerous one, and you need to understand that there's no one on this team willing to explain to your mother that we have elected to tape your broken ribs so that you can play football. Tony, you may not know it yet, but there's a Busia (grandmother) team out there in East Hammond made up of our mothers and some of the older women like Mrs. Jebronovich and Mrs. Malakovich. They tolerate our football and boxing. We start taping broken ribs and such to play football, and we piss them off. Then they form a coalition with the Polish nuns at St. Mary's who taught all of us, and we are dead meat. You get my drift, Tony?"

Saint Mary's Franciscan Sisters
of Blessed Kunegunda

Tony, eyes wide and looking straight at Fatty, said, "OK, Fatty, I get it, I get it." Walt, sensing Tony's embarrassment, looked up at Tony and said, "Tony, every guy in this room knows how much you love this game, and we also know you played the last half of our last game with those broken ribs. You're a hell of a football player and really important to our team next year so get well, kid."

Fatty nodded and Tony said, "Thanks, Walt. Thanks, Fatty. Thanks, guys." As he looked at the team, "I'll get well."

For the next half hour Fatty completed the list. Mike Malakovich out for Cal City, possibly Chicago Heights due to a pulled hamstring. Walter Kwolek out for the Cal City game, possibly Chicago Heights due to a badly sprained right ankle. Finally, Pete Mindok out for the Cal City game, had already missed last game due to a badly sprained left shoulder. Could possibly be ready for the Chicago Heights game.

After Fatty finished, Walt took over.

"OK, guys. Listen up. This is the starting line up for the Cal City game this Sunday: Chet Jasinski at quarterback. Lefty Golarz at right halfback. Novalik at fullback. Heinie Milobar at right end. George Stoming at left end. Kal Borbely at center.

Alex Fyda and Johnny Gorski at guards. Budnyk and Pulkowski at tackles, and finally myself at left halfback. The rest of you guys—Golec, Enock and Dotlich—be ready to play because you'll be in there a lot. Those guys out due to injuries be on the truck to the game with the rest of us on Sunday. Remember, we leave here as usual from Wusic's garage at 12:30 p.m. Fatty or anybody got anything to add?"

Walt looked around and waited, but no one said anything. Finally, Walt concluded, "Sorry for the long meeting but we needed it. See you all on Sunday, if not before."

The meeting adjourned and the team began to leave. All appeared to be in pretty good spirits.

Playing Calumet City

It was Sunday, November 4, 1934, and game day with Calumet City. The weather had taken a cold turn on Friday, November 2. There had, as yet, been no precipitation, but that was now changing. Weather predictions for game time were 25 degrees, a strong southerly wind off of Lake Michigan and lake effect snow which no one was willing to predict in terms of amount.

The Yellow Jackets were at Wusic's and boarding Mike's truck for the ride over to Cal City.

Alex Fyda commented to Mike Wusic, "Hey Mike, are those all the tarps we have?"

"Yeah, Alex. Remember this summer we ran over a couple of the bigger ones and tore the hell out of 'em?"

"Where are they now?"

"On some boards up in the garage."

Lefty chimed in," Well, get 'em, Mike. We'll help ya, even if they're tore to hell, they're better than those few small ones in the back of this open truck."

By this time everyone was finding a spot in the flat bed as Wusic, Lefty, and Alex brought out the big torn tarps that were quickly spread over twenty guys trying to keep warm.

The ride over to Cal City was cold but reasonably short–about a half hour. They traveled west down 165th Street, which became 159th Street in Illinois. They then continued on 159th to Burnham Avenue and then North on Burnham all the way to the commercial area of Cal City and the Field. Of all the teams that the Yellow Jackets played, the team that had, by far, the worst field was Cal City. The field was normally used by a trucking company to park their trucks. On these game days, they would move their trucks in sufficient numbers to provide an area for a football game, a hard, rocky, grassless surface that Cal City called their home field. Cal City was to line the field. Typically, however, this task wasn't done very well. Consequently, whether or not a team got a first down was often left to the discretion of the ref who would judge ten yards by his eye. The one positive about Cal City was that they always had a crowd, and today would be no exception, regardless of the impending bad weather.

Cal City this year had a great team, having lost only once, and that loss, 7 to 6, was to the perennial powerhouse Hegewisch who remained undefeated and whom the Yellow Jackets would not play this year. The Yellow Jackets came to this game for the season with six wins and no losses, but battered and bruised; whereas, Cal City had nearly an injury free season.

As the Yellow Jacket truck pulled in, it was readily apparent that the crowd of some 1500 was already in an ugly, loud, alcohol-drinking mood. Several beer bottles hit the truck as they moved to where they had been directed to park. From every direction the Yellow Jackets could hear vulgarities and profanities being shouted at them. Several of the younger players appeared nervous.

Lefty Golarz noticing this, looked over at his young teammates and said in a loud voice, "Hey Guys, don't let that bother ya. If it gets any worse, I will personally get out of this truck and kick the shit out of every one of 'em."

There was a brief moment of silence and then spontaneously the entire truck of Yellow Jackets broke into laughter and in that moment they were ready to play a football game – really ready.

The weather was deteriorating. It was getting windier, and the snow, though still light, was racing across the playing field.

The coin-toss resulted in Cal City kicking off to the Yellow Jackets. The teams positioned themselves on the field. The ref blew his whistle. The ball was kicked low, over the heads of the Yellow Jackets, hitting around the 25 yard line, then took a fast bounce to the 20 where Lefty, already on a risky dead run, grabbed it. He ran straight up the middle to about the 30, then made a very quick cut to his right, avoiding two potential tacklers A split second after his cut, Alex Fyda made a bone-crushing hit at the 40 yard line on a big lineman his size who never saw it coming. The crowd made a deep groan. Lefty then sped past the 40 toward the 50 yard line and the sideline. Another evasive move and he was at Cal City's 40-yard line.

Then, notwithstanding Alex Fyda's great hit, came the downfield block of the entire game. As Lefty reached Cal City's 30 yard line, a quick-moving potential tackler stood in his way. Lefty cut to the inside. The tackler, focusing on Lefty, did not see the 205 pound Pulkowski. Lefty cut back to the outside and the poor kid belonged to Pulkowski. The hit was a full-frontal hit, both extraordinary and frightening, and despite the strong wind you could hear the crack all over the field. Lefty sprinted untouched the remainder of the way into the end zone. The kid never returned to the game. The ugly crowd was silent. Walt kicked the extra point. The score was Yellow Jackets 7, Calumet City 0. Fourteen seconds of the game had elapsed.

The wind and snow were now increasing in intensity, the wind howling and the snow becoming that heavier and thicker snow that all who have lived south of the Great Lakes recognize as lake effect.

The Yellow Jackets kicked off. Cal City caught the ball on the 15 yard line, but the ball carrier was hit almost immediately by Heinie Milobar and George Stoming. Cal City, reeling from the quick Yellow Jacket score, was attempting to shake it off and come back. They were having some success running up the middle on the Yellow Jackets. They had secured one first down and were working on another. It was third and one on the 34 yard line when their quarterback, hampered by freezing hands, dropped the snap, and the ball fell to the ground where Kal Borbely immediately fell on it, then with both hands pulled it to his chest. Yellow Jacket ball on the 35 yard line.

The Yellow Jackets called a time out. Fatty Grisha came out with water, but only a few wanted it. Chester Jasinski got on one knee, looked up at the huddled team and said, "Guys, we can break their backs right here."

Walt looked at him and said, "Tell us what you got, Chet."

"They're gonna be lookin' for Lefty, so I fake a pitch to Lefty around the right end. Then I hand off to you, Walt, right on Lefty's ass. Anyone comin' that way from Cal City is fresh meat for Lefty."

Walt looked at Lefty. Lefty smiled and said, "Let's do it."

The Yellow Jackets then lined up. Chet called out his signal. Kal snapped the ball. Chet faked the pitch then made his hand-off. Lefty hit their end with a crushing block and then took out the linebacker. Walt, tight behind Lefty, sped 35 yards to the end zone. The Yellow Jackets kicked the extra point and the score was Yellow Jackets 14, Cal City 0.

The wind was now fierce and would remain so for the rest of the game. The snow was taking hold and covering everything including the field.

The crowd was silent and feeling even colder than it was. A few had begun to leave. Most would be gone before the end of the game.

After that quick second score, Chet was right. Much of Cal City's will was gone, and throughout the game it wouldn't improve. Oh, there was an occasional punch thrown, an occasional late hit, but for the most part, the Yellow Jackets were playing a defeated team. The latter part of the game was harder on the Yellow Jackets than Cal City. There's not much fun in engaging someone who either can't or won't fight back. Cal City had met the 1934 Yellow Jackets. But it wasn't fun. Final score: Yellow Jackets 35, Calumet City 0.

The Yellow Jackets headed for the truck. Walt, Lefty and Pulkowski made a quick trip to the Cal City side of the field to check on the kid who never made it back after Pulkowski's hit. Then they too headed for the truck. Normally, there's some chatter and laughter on the truck ride home, especially after a good win, but this ride home was just cold and quiet. A good win requires two teams who fight to the bitter end, and that didn't happen. So everyone quietly was just trying to get under that part of the tarp that didn't have a hole in it.

Coal From The Tracks

Early cold weather for the East Hammond community in the mid-thirties of the Depression was not a good thing, especially if it was not just a cold snap but meant an early beginning to a long winter. Homes were heated with coal and the cost of a ton of coal, even a half a ton, was almost prohibitive to a family focused on simply trying to put food on the table. So, in 1934, when the temperature dropped into the twenties in early November and stayed there, people, especially children and the old, were cold in their homes.

A number of homes had a wood-burning pot-bellied stove. This stove was often in the kitchen, but, though much better than nothing, proved inadequate for a normal house with two or three bedrooms. The Grelak family on Ames Avenue, as an example, had such a stove, but by the time full winter came with temperatures in the teens and below, the wood stove was not sufficient.

East Hammond families lived on the edge of destitution. There was never enough money for anything and food always loomed as the primary need until it got so cold that you could find little comfort anywhere in your own home. There was at that time in Hammond, as well as in other American communities of those times, agencies funded by taxes and voluntary contributions to tend to the needs of the poor. Most Americans of this time, including the citizens of East Hammond, were reluctant to go begging to these organizations for they were proud people. Usually, these organizations were set up in a manner whereby those requesting help needed to stand in long lines, then fill out a set of forms, then sit and wait for their names, usually mispronounced, to be shouted out so that the nearly 100 other "beggars" in the room could hear. Such was the customary procedures in the Township Trustee's Office, or the General Relief Agency, or the host of smaller agencies whose partial purpose was to serve the needs of the poor. The staffs of these agencies were usually marginally educated and had often gotten their jobs because they knew someone. They were overworked and their manner, therefore, was often crass and degrading to the "beggar" already in a state of extreme humiliation. Little wonder that most poor would declare, "I'll starve before I go beggin' to those sons-of-bitches." Nonetheless, when someone of the poor did manage to make it through this less than perfect and often dehumanizing process, the reward usually was a voucher for a quarter or half-ton of coal, a dollar to three dollar food voucher, or a voucher for a child's coat or a pair of shoes.

When the Depression came, an emerging practice that we might call "coal from the tracks" began to occur. As fuel for heating homes became unaffordable, the poor throughout America found that pieces of coal often lay along the railroad tracks of our country, having fallen off the trains that were over the years, moving coal. Collecting this coal either in baskets or sacks became a common practice of the poor, usually done by the children. As engineers of trains observed these children, they were known to attempt to assist them out of their own sense of empathy. They would do so occasionally by actually shoveling coal out of box cars. More commonly, with their train traveling through a community, they would brake suddenly their 40 to 100 box car coal trains in such a way that the entire train and all its box cars would shudder. This would cause coal to fall off along a mile or two stretch of track. The engineers knew which section of track on their routes had poor who collected coal for they saw them.

East Hammond had such a stretch of track along both its northern and western boundaries and its residents knew that periodically, about twice a month, engineers would shudder their train to provide for this coal fall-off. The tracks, however, were on private property, thus there grew an understanding between law enforcement agents and the citizens of East Hammond that such collecting must be done discretely. Otherwise, they would run the risk of being arrested and this was a condition law enforcement would prefer to avoid. The practice of collection, therefore, often became a night time event and fell to older family children.

"Lefty...Lefty...Lefty," repeated Kal Borbely in his loud whisper voice as he threw small pebbles against Lefty and Walt Golarz's bedroom window from the yard below.

The window opened and Lefty leaned out. "What the hell you doin,' Kal?"

"It's almost 2:00 a.m. and we said we're all leavin' to go to the tracks at 2:00 a.m.," Kal replied.

"It's ten to two, Kal, ten to two. I'm putting on my pants. Walt and I will be out there right away," Lefty said impatiently and slammed the window shut.

Alex Fyda said to Kal, "I think you pissed him off."

"He'll be all right," Kal assured him.

Seven or eight Yellow Jackets had gathered in the Golarz back yard by the time Walt and Lefty came out of the back door of the house.

Walt asked, "Where's everybody else?"

Alex Fyda explained, "They're all meeting at Milobar's and walkin' to the tracks about a half-mile west of Hammond High School. Then they're gonna come back south, collecting coal along the tracks and meeting us at about the ice house,"

"Okay, gotcha, good plan," says Walt, "then we don't have too many guys workin' the same stretch of track".

Alex told Walt, "It wasn't my idea."

Walt replied, "It doesn't matter, Alex. It's a good plan."

The group with their burlap bags, baskets and buckets, walked to Columbia Avenue, then south to the tracks near the cemetery south of 165th, then southeast along the tracks for about a half a mile. As they walked along the tracks with their lanterns and flashlights, they saw quite a bit of coal.

Walt cautioned, "Don't pick it up yet, guys. We'll get it when we turn to go back."

Finally they reached a point near Indianapolis Boulevard and Walt said, "Okay, guys, let's fill up our bags and buckets and head back."

As they headed back, they were surprised to find more coal than they were used to seeing. Johnny Topolski exclaimed, "Hey, we're not going to have enough bags and baskets if this keeps up."

Then Walt spoke up, "That's good, Johnny. We've got a lot of cold old-timers and kids in the neighborhood. By the way, any of you guys have any special requests from your folks?"

George Stoming replied, "Yeah, Walt. My folks told me not to forget old Mrs. Jubronovich."

Lefty commented to George and the others, "I think Heinie has that covered, but I'm not sure."

Walt added, "When we meet up with our guys comin' up the tracks, we'll ask him."

The collecting was good that night and indeed Heinie was taking care of Mrs. Jubronovich. By 4:00

a.m. all the coal they collected had been delivered to their respective homes and also to two more of what Walt called "special requests." Despite the cold, from 4:00 a.m. to 6:00 a.m. a second load was successfully collected and delivered. Throughout the winter they would periodically perform this night time ritual until such time as the warmth came with the spring. But right now it was 6:15 a.m., and they were on their way to Wusic's for a cup of coffee and an hour or so of comraderie and a chance for Lefty to tease Kal Borbely about 1:50 a.m. and how that's different than 2:00 a.m. There really wasn't enough for any of them to have a full cup of coffee, so they carefully never took one. But then they never really needed a full cup, for when they were together at times like this, despite what they lacked, they always understood that their lives, because of one another, were full and their cups truly did "runneth over."

A Very Dangerous Opponent

It was the last game of the season and the Yellow Jackets were 7-0. They had won all of their games but had taken a beating with injuries along the way. For this last game against Chicago Heights they would still have five guys out. The beating that they had given to Calumet City two weeks earlier was still being talked about in the Northwest Indiana/South Chicago football community. The Yellow Jackets were actually being viewed by some as a potential competitor for the Chicago Bears. All of this talk did not sit well, particularly with Walt and Fatty. They were focused on Chicago Heights. Chicago Heights was coming into this game with three losses, including a 7-6 loss to Calumet City, the team that the Yellow Jackets had just embarrassed. But those other two losses were one point losses to Hegewisch and Joliet

State Prison. Walt and Fatty were really the only two guys who knew the Joliet State Prison team. In the 1932 season, Walt's first year on the Yellow Jackets, Joliet Prison was their only loss, 14 to 0. But Walt remembers that it could have been much worse, for Joliet let up in the second half. Actually, in Walt and Fatty's opinion, if there was a team in the greater Chicagoland area that could play at the level of the Bears, it would be Joliet Prison. Therefore, for Fatty and Walt, the team getting off of the bus right now on the far side of the Yellow Jacket field was dangerous—very dangerous.

For players, the conditions for playing a football game were nothing short of ideal. It was a bright, sunny, late November day with little wind and a temperature of about 50 degrees. Although it was predicted that the temperature by evening would drop and continue dropping throughout the night, at the moment weather conditions were perfect for football. Even the field looked its Sunday best with the exception of the rock pile in the southwest corner—a massive pile of bricks and houseblocks left over from the demolition of the company houses that years earlier stood in this area. On Saturday, Lefty, Kal Borbely and Heinie Milobar had lined the field with lye donated by old man Jebroski. They had done an exceptionally good job and the field looked ready. The Yellow Jackets only hoped that it would be a great hard fought game worthy of a final victory. Little did they know that the game they would soon play that clear November afternoon would test to the limit all of their strength, determination, skill, and will to win as a team and as individuals.

Make-shift seating was being constructed by hundreds of old timers from two by sixes and house bricks they had carried down the streets from the east Hammond neighborhood that spread north and south along Columbia Avenue which ran parallel to the field. While they constructed, still countless arrivals were beginning to pour in from the neighborhood. They came from Conkey Street, Ames, Moss, Kenwood, Cleveland, 163rd and beyond. There were the Busias with their bubushkas covering their hair, kids of all ages, young men, mothers with baby buggies, hopeful young women and a continual endless stream of more old-timers all in their white shirts, ties and hats. Unlike most previous home games, this game was also drawing a great number of football enthusiasts from far beyond Hammond. Consequently, hundreds of cars were lined on

Colombia Avenue all the way back to 165th Street and south. Furthermore, any space adjacent to the field for a hundred yards back to the fence, that was the boundary for Pullman Standard, was being used by someone for parking. Later estimates would judge the number who came to see this game between 2,000 and 2,500.

As the time of the game approached, Walt, Fatty Grisha, and Mike Wusic were scrambling through the crowd trying to assemble their team. They found a number of them surrounded, in small groups, by excited and adoring fans. Some of their players they just couldn't locate. The noise and excitement was not unlike the midway at a fair or circus. As they continued to gather their team, one of the three refs found Fatty, pulled him aside, and warned him that 2:00 p.m. game time had passed and that according to his watch it was now 2:05 p.m., and he would give the Yellow Jackets only until 2:10 p.m. to be on the field and ready to play. After 2:10 p.m. he would assess a 15 yard penalty on the kick off. Further, he advised Fatty and Walt who had just joined them that if the Yellow Jackets were still not on the field at 2:15 pm they would forfeit the game.

Mike Wusic then arrived with Alex Fyda and Lefty.

Walt said quickly, "Lefty, you and Alex get out to the field for the coin-toss." As they left running, Walt turned to Fatty and Wusic and said, "We got at least eight guys right here. I don't care who they are or what position they are used to playing, just get 'em out on that field. With me, Lefty and Fyda, that makes eleven. Let's go play football." Out on the field the coin-toss had taken place. Chicago Heights won the toss and elected to receive. Walt, with a full complement of players, kicked off. It was a typical "Walt" kick that went sailing to the back of the end zone. There was no return and the ball came out to the 20 yard line. As this was occurring, several Yellow Jacket substitutions were taking place by genuinely embarrassed starters.

As Chicago Heights broke and came to the line for their first play, Walt, from his inside linebacker position yelled out to his team, "OK, gentlemen, we're in a football game now."

If a football game is that which will test your limits, then Walt's words to his team were prophetic, for in the next 60 minutes of play the Yellow Jackets, each and all, would be tested.

Preseason Chicago Heights had a fullback named Stanley Wojekowski who had broken all rushing records in the South Chicagoland area of play the year before. The Yellow Jackets and others who followed Chicagoland football had understood that he was unable to play this year because of severe reoccurring hamstring problems. This was a blessing for opponents, since the 195- pound, six-foot-two Wojekowski was considered by most who had watched him play as fairly invincible. So, as Walt looked past their center and then past their quarterback and into the eyes of their fullback, he knew with all the instincts of a longtime veteran who he was looking at. Walt made a quick glance to Lefty on his right, and Lefty glanced at Walt then nodded. Both veterans knew and were preparing for a long, hard-fought afternoon.

The Chicago Heights quarterback set, looked around, called his signals, and the ball was snapped. Their line, with quick and hard-hitting execution, opened a hole off tackle. The quarterback faked a hand-off to Wojekowski who sped through the hole like a halfback, cut inside, and headed right for Walt. Walt had actually been positioning himself to take on Wojekowski, assuming he would have the ball. Their strategy worked and Wojekowski delivered a great block, neutralizing Walt. Then right behind Wojekowski, came a very fast half back who had the ball. He stayed with Wojekowski till the block on Walt, then cut. Lefty was lucky to hit him after a five yard gain.

In that one play, Chicago Heights had revealed their game plan for the afternoon. Dominate up front, use Wojekowski primarily to block as he came through the hole first, then hand off to one of their half backs, or have the quarterback fake twice, keep the ball, and come through the hole himself with the two backs right ahead of him. Their execution was flawless and the Yellow Jackets were back on their heels. Within four minutes, Chicago Heights had moved down the field of play four to six yards at a crack. They never threw the ball. They just moved like a great machine, cutting down whatever was in its way to the Yellow Jacket seven yard line. By this time, the home crowd was virtually silent. They weren't used to this. They weren't used to their Yellow Jackets being outplayed, for that was what was happening. Chicago Heights was out-blocking, out-hitting, and out-executing the Yellow Jackets. They moved without wasted motion, and play after play, looked like a team of one—not eleven separate players.

They were playing with confidence and skill. They were playing the way East Hammond was used to seeing their Yellow Jackets play.

On the next play, Wojekowski, without any blocking, went off tackle, knocking over two of the Yellow Jackets defensive linemen, then cutting to the outside and in for the score. The score was Chicago Heights 6, Yellow Jackets 0. The point after was missed.

The kick off by Chicago Heights went into the end zone. There was no return and the Yellow Jackets took the ball of the twenty yard line. The next three plays may have been the most humiliating of the game for the Yellow Jackets. The first play from scrimmage was a hand off to Lefty who was hit hard in the backfield as he got the ball. The second play to Walt resulted in a tackle for loss. The third play to Novalik again resulted in a tackle for loss.

It was now fourth and seven on the Yellow Jacket thirteen yard line. Lefty got off a good punt which was fielded on their 38 yard line by one of their scat backs who quickly ran right up the middle to the 50 where a host of Yellow Jackets were prepared and poised to take him down. Then, out of nowhere, Wojekowski, running toward the sideline, came in behind his running back. The running back stopped dead in his tracks and did a quick pitch back to Wojekowski who sped to the sideline and then rounded the Yellow Jacket team and continued untouched to the end zone. The score was now Chicago Heights 12, Yellow Jackets 0. The point after was good, making the score 13 to nothing. The crowd was dead silent. The Yellow Jackets, who to this point in the season, hadn't had anyone score two touchdowns on them in an entire game, were down 13 to nothing, and it was still the first quarter.

Walt called a time out. Fatty came out on the field with Mike Wusic. Walt looked at Lefty and the team, and then said to all of them, "You guys remember two weeks ago in Cal City? First quarter and we had broken their backs. Is that where we are? Is that all that we have left—an occasional punch or an occasional late hit? Are they saying to themselves right now that we are a team that either can't or won't fight back? Is this two weeks ago, but now we're Cal City?"

Lefty stood up and in a loud voice shouted to the team. "This is bullshit, guys. We can't let 'em kick the shit out of us. Let's go."

With some renewed enthusiasm the Yellow Jackets took their positions and Chicago Heights kicked off. The second quarter continued to belong to Chicago Heights. Only because of a fumble as Chicago Heights was attempting to score at the end of the second quarter, did the score remain 13 to 0.

Mrs. Pulkowski

The half time break was a blessing for the Yellow Jackets. They were tired and being outplayed in every aspect of the game. They were being out tackled, out blocked, and they were playing a team that seemed to know that they would win. They were playing a team that was playing with confidence, and at the moment confidence is what the Yellow Jackets were in short supply of.

As they sat there together with Fatty trying to encourage them, trying to ignite the spark, the clock was ticking to the beginning of the second half. Then an unusual and unexpected thing happened. Walking purposefully through the crowd and directly toward the gathered Yellow Jacket team came Pulkowski's mother. Her attire completed in every aspect the classic look of a 1935 East Hammond Busia (grandmother) from the babushka covering her grey hair to the black plain purse she carried with a strap over the shoulder, to the dark overcoat that had large buttons and came down below her knees. She was a short, husky woman. Her hands were gloveless and were thick and appeared strong. Hands that had seen a lifetime of work. If you could have gotten into her purse, you would have found a little change purse, a clean white handkerchief, a small mirror, a little comb, and a rosary, probably black. Her shoes were dark and flat on the bottom and she wore dark brown cotton stockings. She walked with an air of purpose and quiet authority. And this day she came to the edge of the gathered Yellow Jackets, stopped, looked around, spotted her son sitting on the ground and in a loud voice, but not a shout, called to him in her less than perfect English, "Saw nee" (sonny). Pulkowski, immediately recognizing her voice and startled by her presence, walked toward her and responded, "Yeah, Ma."

Then quietly he asked her in Polish, "Ma, why are you here?"

She corrected him speaking in her phonetically imperfect and somewhat choppy English, complete with rolling "r's" and said, "You tawk de English now." Polkowski responded sheepishly, "Well, what, Ma?"

By this time, she had the undivided attention of the entire team, including Fatty and Wusic. She had come with her brother Hugo from Hegewisch to watch her son win a game, and she was very upset and embarrassed, so she then said as she stood looking right up into Pulkowski's face, "Vats a madda you? Uncle Hugo come frrrom de Hegevish place tuh brrring meh tuh sih you beh vin, but you not beh vin. You beh loose! Soh! I come dis place tuh tell you I beh herre tuh sih you beh vin. Soh! you go vin! Now!"

Pulkowski tried to speak, but she stopped him. "You beh not tawk. You beh vin!" She then turned and left.

Pulkowski just stood there for a long moment then turned and looked at Walt, Fatty, Wusic, and the team. Then he said, "Shit...I don't know about you guys, but I just got my marching orders, and if you didn't notice, I think she was talkin' to you guys too."

They all ran off with an enthusiasm that Walt and Fatty had not seen all day. A different team was coming back to the field.

Walt turned to Fatty and said quietly, "We got any more busias out there?"

A Fragile Thread

To begin the second half, Chicago Heights kicked to the back of the end zone. Lefty fielded it and began to run it back. At about the 15 yard line, the crowd could see Wojekowski with a great angle on Lefty. What Wojekowski did not see was Pulkowski coming full-bore with a perfect angle on him. The hit was solid and Wojekowski flew through the air. The entire crowd responded with a loud cheer which became a sustained cheer that had been building up for the entire first half. Lefty continued past the 50 and to about the 35 yard line of Chicago Heights where he was finally brought down. Pulkowski had ignited the spark. Lefty had a great run. The Yellow Jackets were on the 35 yard line of Chicago Heights, and the crowd was alive.

Lefty

In the huddle, Chet Jasinski, overflowing with enthusiasm, said, "The right play and we're back in the game."

Walt replied, "Okay, Chet, whatcha got?"

Chet responded, "Our second touchdown at Cal City."

Then both Chet and Walt looked at Lefty who simply nodded and said, "I'm ready. Let's go."

Chet was right. He faked the pitch to Lefty, then the hand-off to Walt who came behind Lefty, who was now throwing defenders aside left and right. Walt simply gained speed and was moving like a freight train at full throttle. Only a 150 pound, wide-eyed, flat-footed safety with his arms outstretched stood in Walt's way. Talk about giving your all for the cause. Walt hit the kid viciously and then was into the end zone still at full speed as if there had been no obstacle at all in his way. The score was now Yellow Jackets 6, Chicago Heights 13. Walt kicked the extra point and the score was 7 to 13. The crowd was ecstatic. They had come to see their Yellow Jackets and in two plays there they were.

Chicago Heights, however, was not a team that was going to roll over. They had been caught off guard by a team that had regained its will and resolve. But, they had lost none of theirs, so it would be a dog fight in the middle of that field for the next two quarters. The game of football, at its best, is two really good teams playing at the top of their wills and abilities: great tackling, blocking, running, crisp and sharp playing, few mistakes, a handful of really great plays, and a group of young men who have a commitment to team. In late November, 1934, in the afternoon, on the Hammond Yellow Jacket field, this is what a community of football fans were given as a gift from these young men. They were given a gift to watch and remember: a great game of football.

But, now it was the fourth quarter with less than a minute to play and the score was still Yellow Jackets 7, Chicago Heights 13. The Yellow Jacket defense had again stopped Chicago Heights, forcing them to punt on fourth down. The punt was a good one, putting the Yellow Jackets on their own 30 yard line, a full 70 yards from the end zone and 37 seconds left to play.

To this point, most of the Yellow Jackets offensive plays had been running plays with the exception of two successful short passes. One thrown by Lefty to Heinie and one thrown by Chet to Lefty. Walt called a time out. All afternoon Lefty had told Walt and Chet that if they needed a long pass, he was sure he could come out of the back field and run past their linebackers and be open at mid field. The Yellow Jackets huddled. Chet and Walt looked at Lefty and said, "You ready for that pass, Left?"

Lefty smiled and nodded. Chet could always throw a good ball, but this one was one of his best, and Lefty was there, right past the linebackers where Lefty caught the ball as it came over his left shoulder. Now the 50 yard line, the 40, the 30, and Lefty was hit and down on the 27. Every person in the stands and surrounding the field were on their feet. The noise from the crowd was intense. Time was running and Walt called their last time out. Seventeen seconds remained in the game.

They huddled and Walt said, "All right, guys, this whole second half we have played them with great, hard football. We've matched or beat them, tackle for tackle, and block for block. Now in this last 17 seconds we're gonna win this game by being smarter than they are."

Then Walt looked at Chet, "Chet, if I tell you to have George, Hienie and Lefty all go out, down, and to the RIGHT…"

Chet interrupts, "Walt, that won't work, they will flood that area with all of their safeties and linebackers, and ..."

Walt interrupts, "That's right, Chet, that's why I want you to throw that pass out of bounds. Then with time remaining for our last play have them all go out and to the LEFT and..."

Chet smiles and interrupts, The Statute of Liberty play."

Walt smiles and says, "You're a bright guy, Chester. Let's just pray that Wojekowski and company aren't as smart as you.

As Walt predicted, the passing play had Chicago Heights flood the area with defenders and Chester threw the pass away. Now the last six seconds of the game. Kal Borbely snapped the ball. Chester dropped back. He grabbed the ball with two hands as if he were going to throw, then using his non-throwing hand, he dropped his hand down and behind his back with the ball. Meanwhile, with his empty throwing hand, he pump-faked a throw to the left corner of the field where Lefty, George and Heinie were arriving, followed by the entire secondary and core of linebackers from Chicago Heights. Then, simultaneously, Chet handed the ball off to Walt who, in motion, ran past his back and in the direction of the right corner of the field. With the ball in hand, Walt came blazing around the right corner of the line. He got all the way to the 20 yard line before even being seen by the cluster of Chicago Heights players in the left corner with Lefty, Heinie, and George. As Chicago Heights players watched Walt, they knew it was too late. Walt ran untouched into the end zone. The execution of the play was carried out at its deceptive best. Amos Alonzo Stagg and Clarence Herschberger of the University of Chicago would have been proud. Walt kicked the extra point and the score was Yellow Jackets 14, Chicago Heights 13.

The crowd could not be contained. They ran onto the field, jumping, hugging, screaming, dancing, and feeling just purely joyful. The Yellow Jackets had finished the season without a defeat. They knew though that the Chicago Heights team had taught them in those sixty minutes a lifelong lesson: the distance between winning and losing can be and often is a fragile thread.

A Festive Community

The game was over, but the crowd didn't want to leave. Many who had come from a distance and had driven were pulling away and getting caught in a rare traffic jam, but those from East Hammond were still milling around in large and small groups. Some were beginning to move back to the neighborhood and a fairly large number were heading to Wusic's gas station. Eventually, all of the team would be at Wusic's, for most would do some partial changing of their clothes there, putting on at least a dry skivvy shirt before they headed for home. The day was still pleasant enough for standing and talking. The temperature at this point had only dropped to about 45 degrees.

As evening neared and the night cold came in, only the hardy, young, and older football fanatics would remain. Most would be near the gas station, having captured one or two of their favorite players and enthusiastically engaging them in a conversation about some aspect of the game. Other fans didn't have football as their agenda. Such as the small clusters of attractive young East Hammond women who were interested in one or more of the players. The Yellow Jackets selected for such attention did not seem to mind. Lefty and Kal Borbely, for example, seemed quite content with the attention they were receiving from "Gigs"(Helen Grelak) and Mary Bindas of Ames Street. Other players were a bit less fortunate, having been trapped by clusters of old-timers intent on reminiscing about the great games of the twenties. But, regardless of from where the attention came, it was good.

Normally, at about 5:30 or 6:00 p.m. after a home game, Fatty and Walt would coax the players into the Yellow Jacket room for a brief team meeting. But, as they looked out at the crowd still gathered and sensed the continued festive atmosphere, they judged that the meeting could wait, if for nothing more than to give Mrs. Pulkowski time to introduce her brother Hugo to all of East Hammond. The Yellow Jackets were enjoying their community and their community was enjoying them. Let the festivities continue. It had been a long, hard-fought season.

Joining the Calumet Region Football League

It was late November and the Yellow Jackets were gathered for a team meeting. There was a light snow outside and someone had started a fire in the small wood-burning stove. Soon they could take their jackets or sweaters off and enjoy the warmth.

Fatty stood near the chalkboard and said, "Guys, we asked you here today because something has come up that we all need to make a decision about. As you know, right after our last game, the mayor and some city officials, as well as some business men, asked us to bring a small group to city hall in the mayor's office to listen to a proposal. I asked Walt, Lefty, Heinie, Kal, and Pulkowski to go with me. I asked if any of the others of you felt like you wanted to be there, but everyone said they were comfortable with the group going and simply asked that you later be told what was going on. I know that you have all since been brought up to date, one on one by the guys who went. Nonetheless, we needed this meeting. The proposal these people made to us was to ask us to join a new football league that they are planning to form next year. The Yellow Jackets have since our beginning in 1931 been independent. We have set our own schedule, paid our own way, taken care of our own equipment, our own uniforms, and our own lettermen's sweaters. The little money we have gotten from passing the hat at games we have used to pay refs, occasionally buy a football, repair Wusic's truck, give something to the opposing team, and pay for gas to away games. Once in awhile there were a few bucks left over, and we split it evenly, twenty-two ways. By the way, that last game left us more money than we have ever seen, so each guy gets $3.05, and you get it today."

A cheer went up in the room.

Lefty then got up and announced, "Just so it's out in the open, I'm one of the guys opposed to this league. I just don't trust it, but if the majority of you guys want to try it, I'll be with you."

Kal Borbely added a second to Lefty's comment.

Mike Dotlich then asked, "Fatty, why would we want to do this?"

"Well, Mike, first they will cover all equipment costs. Second, they will see to it that fields are lined by them. Third, the teams we play won't be as far as Joliet, or Warsaw, or Lafayette. They will be closer and that's less wear and tear on Wusic's truck. Fourth, if somebody gets hurt, they will help cover doctor costs, and finally, more of our East Hammond people can get to our away games because they will be closer."

Alex Fyda spoke up, "Fatty, do you know who some of the other teams will be in this league?"

"Well, here's what we've been told.. The Indiana Harbor Night Hawks, The East Chicago Blue Eagles, Lansing, a new team from Hessville, and a new team from Hammond, and as you can see there is still some room in a normal schedule for a couple of games outside of the league that we could decide on. Anybody else got a comment or question?"

Johnny Gorski asked, "If we decide to do this, for how long are we committed?"

"They want us long term, but they will welcome us even if we tell 'em we're only willing to try it for one year. Anybody else?"

The room was silent, and Fatty then said, "Guys, those were good questions. Now, let me turn it over to Walt."

Walt took over, "Okay, guys, we're not doin' any more on this today. Talk to one another, mull it over in your own head, give it some time. Next week on Thursday at 4:00 p.m. right here at Wusic's, we vote. If the majority want to try it, then we do it, and if the majority don't want to, then we stay independent. See ya next Thursday, if not before."

The following Thursday in early December the Yellow Jackets met and voted. It was a close vote, but a vote to try the league with a commitment for just one year. In 1935 the Hammond Yellow Jackets would be a member of the newly formed Calumet Region Football League.

The Christmas Purse

During the Depression, many of the women of East Hammond did house work for families of means. The homes of these families were in more affluent neighborhoods. Most of these neighborhoods were located west of Hohman Avenue and east of the Indiana/Illinois State Line. Generally, they were approximately two to two and a half miles from the East Hammond community. To get to work a woman from East Hammond had normally only two options. Take a bus that would cost her five cents each way, or walk. The option that was always taken despite the weather or how well she felt was to walk, for that saved her a dime and a dime, at that time, was the price of a loaf of bread. The path of the walk taken was from East Hammond, along the railroads that went northwest toward the downtown area.

Then at an appropriate location she would leave the tracks and head west along one of the several east/west streets until she got to the neighborhood and house where she was employed.

House cleaning work was sought after. It was clean, in pleasant surroundings, and consistent in pay for usually two to three days per week. Although it paid only about 15 cents per hour, an average week's pay of approximately $3.00 paid for a family's weekly food and sometimes also a pair of shoes or such. Most men at that time were unemployed, so the house work money of the mother and daughters, if a household had a daughter who could also work, provided the primary and often only source of family income. Young men could sometimes find part time work, but those jobs were scarce at best.

The date was Friday, December 21, 1934, three days before the Polish Wigilia (the Christmas Eve traditional meal). It was 6:15 p.m. and the temperature outside was 18 degrees and it was quite windy. Ma Golarz was very late coming home from work. Walt, Lefty, and Pa were getting very nervous. On Fridays she was normally home by 3:30 p.m. Lefty was getting dressed to go out looking for her. At that moment the back door

72

opened and Ma, tripping on the top step, fell into the kitchen with a horrendous thud. She was a short, stout woman, having much the look of Mrs. Pulkowski. As she fell, Lefty and Wolf were almost immediately by her side. Pa and their younger sister Anne came rushing from the living room a moment later. As they lifted her, they could feel that her hands were icy cold and see that they were bleeding. Further, blood was running down the front of both legs from her knees that were badly scratched, bruised, and dirty. She had somewhere lost her head scarf and her hair was in a total state of disarray, her face beet-red and dirty, while her ears felt frozen. She looked up, crying. At that moment, Pa gently pushed his two sons aside, and lifting her into his arms, just looked at her and said quietly and gently, "Mary, Mary." He held her there for a while in the kitchen, then turned to Walt and directed him to make a comfortable place for her in the living room. He then took her there and her daughter Anne tended to her.

When she finally calmed a bit, they asked her what had happened. She explained that on the way home she lost her change purse—the little black one with blue and green flowers that her sister-in-law gave her—and that the change purse contained this week's wages of $3.70, her Christmas Eve meal money. She said she knew she had it when she was on the tracks because just before then she had used her handkerchief to wipe her face and the change purse was in her coat pocket. When she was still on the tracks, but nearer home, she felt for it and it was gone. She said then that she searched and searched, often on her hands and knees, but she couldn't find it. Then it was getting dark so she came home to get a flashlight. She then wept.

Lefty, visibly shaken, looked at his mother and said, "Don't worry, Ma, we'll find it," then to Walt, "Ready?"

Walt responded, "Let's get our coats, a flashlight, and a lantern."

As they walked to the tracks, Lefty and Walt stopped at Kal's house to let him know that they wouldn't be home, alerting Kal that Lefty couldn't get together with him later as they had planned. They also told him what they were about and then proceeded to the tracks where it was cold, windy, and dark. They started with the location where Ma told them she first felt the purse gone. Then slowly, with their flashlight and lantern on, they walked her route northwest to where she would have begun to walk the tracks. They found nothing.

It was now near 8:30 p.m. and quite cold. They turned back and began to retrace their steps. They were a little less confident now.

As they walked, they could see several lights in the distance. Closer they could hear feint talking from the location of the lights that now seemed to be moving in their direction. Shortly thereafter they heard a shout from a voice they immediately recognized to be Kal Borbely's.

"Hey, what you two guys doin' on the tracks? Tryin' to steal coal?"

Lefty responds, "That you, Kal?"

Kal replies, "Who the hell do you think it is—an early Santa Claus with a bunch of elves?"

By this time they were coming upon the group of nine to ten Yellow Jackets. Walt yelled out, "What are all you guys doin' out here?"

Johnny Gorski responded, "We heard that the last engineer who came racing through here shook his train and there are coins all over the damn tracks."

Then, as Johnny approached Walt, "Hi ya, Walt."

Then Walt said to Johnny, "Thanks for coming, Johnny."

Johnny replied, "Hey, bunch of us were just sittin' around a warm fire at Wusic's, just gettin' fat and needing a brisk walk outdoors when Kal told us about your Ma's purse. So, what can we do?"

Walt said, "Well, how about if we all stay together, spread out along the track, and slowly walk the whole distance Ma walked back and forth until we find it."

Gorski agreed, "That's as good a plan as any. Let's do it."

For the next three hours on that cold and windy night, the Yellow Jackets searched along the track for the little flowered purse. Back and forth. Back and forth. Back and forth. It was now nearing midnight when behind Walt and Lefty who were in the lead along the track, Gorski exclaimed, "We found it." Walt and Lefty turned and raced back to where Gorski was standing. Everyone gathered around as Gorski with both of his hands overlapped and cupped together held an overflowing pile of coins, mostly dimes, nickels, and pennies. As Lefty and Walt stood dumbstruck, looking at his hands with this pile of money, Johnny Gorski said, "It's $3.61. Somewhere nine cents fell out of your Ma's purse."

Walt looked up into Johnny's eyes and shaking his head slowly in a gesture meaning no, said, "Johnny, we can't take this money from you guys."

Johnny simply said, "We aren't givin' it to you and Lefty. It's for a little old Polish lady, sitting and praying in your living room that her sons are gonna find her purse with her Christmas meal money like they promised they would."

Lefty just stood there, his arms down at his sides. He was psychologically defenseless. As he looked at Johnny and the others, it was clear that he was having trouble holding it all together. He took a deep breath, swallowed, and shaking his head, just looked at his friends, this band of Yellow Jackets.

At close to 1:00 a.m. that morning, Ma Golarz got her $3.61. She knew it wasn't hers because she had three dollar bills, two quarters, and two dimes in her change purse. But they made her take it. She was never told who specifically was out there that night, but from that day, whenever some Yellow Jackets were in the house, there was a small pot of coffee on the stove.

The little change purse was never found.

Wigilia

Christmas was always a great time. Whether there was or was not enough food did not seem to matter. Maybe it was great because there was an expectation of good times. Maybe it was the old customs and traditions, or maybe the music transported from a distant land that sounded best sung in its natural, foreign tongue, or maybe it was because all those you knew in your East Hammond community also knew, treasured and found joy in their shared customs, traditions, ethnic foods, and music. Maybe it was the church, filled this time of year with its decorations, colored robes and garments and an unending parade of ceremonies with incense, all of which would culminate in Christmas mass. Maybe it was just all of these things and so, so much more.

It was December 24th, the day before Christmas, and Walt, Lefty, and their kid brother Andy were forcing a big fresh Christmas tree through a front doorway that was fighting back. When they did have a tree for Christmas, it was normally not this grand, but this was the last one that was left on Wusic's truck at the gas station. Mike Wusic occasionally had a way of getting some fresh trees if you didn't mind waiting until December 23rd or so. There had been some smaller trees on the truck, but Walt and Lefty got there late, so, as the saying goes, "you take what you get." By early evening their younger sister Anne, kid brother Andy, and older sister Kate would have the tree decorated. Kate always saw to it that the younger kids would have a new ornament each for the tree. They seemed to like that so.

Pa was sitting in the living room, humming and paging through the 4 ½ by 4½ inch, and two-inch thick Polish Christmas song book, published in Krakow in 1908, a book that he had brought from Poland in 1911 when he came to this country of America alone at the age of fourteen. The book was a favorite of his children who loved to run their fingers over its embossed cover. The cover was a scene of the birth of the Christ Child. It's doubtful that the children could tell you of the scene. They just liked the feel of it. This evening, after the Christmas meal (Wigilia), Pa's song book would be put to good use as family and friends would gather in the dining room and sing, and sing, and sing many of their favorite Christmas carols. They would sing until Pa would judge that it was time to have the children unwrap any gift that someone that day may have laid beneath the tree for them.

Prior to this day, on Saturday, December 22nd, Kate had gone shopping for her mother. There were food items that Mary Golarz needed for the Wigilia meal, but her knees were so bruised and swollen that it was difficult for her to walk. Kate judged that she really couldn't make the shopping trip, even though Zothkiewicz's grocery store on Kenwood Street was only a few blocks away. Kate, therefore, insisted that her mother sit in the living room with her feet up and then advised her that her two daughters could and would tend to whatever needed to be done in the way of preparations before December 24th. Kate knew full-well that there would be no way of keeping her mother out of the kitchen on Christmas Eve for it was a day that Mary Golarz took immense pride in and would not allow anyone to take her place. Kate, of course, would assist her with food preparation, but it would be Mary who would control and direct the preparation of each dish. The meal, as tradition directed, would be meatless and, for Mary, would contain no less than the following: fillets of fish prepared in a butter sauce; herring in oil; a large bowl of seasoned barley; pierogi filled with either potato, cheese, or cabbage; potatoes mashed and buttered; dried fruit; a traditional soup; kapusta (sauerkraut) with mushrooms, and home made breads and sweets.

Once the meal was ready, Mary advised her husband Joe who then directed all present that evening to take a place at a table. Those present that night at the Golarz home were Joe and Mary and their children, Mary's brother and sister-in-law, Mr. and Mrs. Kot, and their two children, and several Yellow Jackets, Kal Borbely, Johnny Gorski, and Alex Fyda. Needless to say, the kitchen table that night was also used to seat people for dinner. Once all were seated, Joe Golarz took a piece of unleavened bread called oplatek, which was purchased for this occasion, broke it, put a small piece in his mouth and passed it on to his wife Mary with a blessing of continued good health.

She, in turn, took a piece and passed it on with a blessing. This was repeated until everyone at the tables had shared in the tradition.

Once this tradition was completed, Mary and her daughter Kate served the meal that had taken since early morning to prepare. That Christmas Eve the joy of that meal was particularly intense, for it represented an unanticipated gift of love which came in the form of a handful of coins from a band of caring young men.

Pa's Polish Christmas song book and
an envelope containing Oplatek

The CCC Camps

Christmas was over as well as the feast day of St. Stephen the Martyr, December 26th. This feast day, particularly for the young people, was always memorable for St. Stephen, the first martyr of the Catholic Church, had been stoned to death. And in his memory, the custom on that day was to come to the house of a friend or neighbor and throw a few nuts at them, announcing the sainthood of St. Stephen. Needless to say, the Yellow Jackets usually overdid the custom, using more than a few nuts and throwing at reckless speed rather than gently, as was the custom's intent. They would then collect the thrown nuts and move on to the next neighbor.

Shortly after the Feast of St. Stephen, Fr. Szezukowski, pastor of St. Mary's, would come to the house on or about the Feast of the Epiphany to bless the House. This was an annual event. He came with an altar boy who carried the holy water. The blessing, with a traditional hymn and the sprinkling of holy water throughout the house, was brief and culminated with Father writing in chalk on the upper interior door frame of the house, the current year and the initials of the three Wise Men: Balthazar, Casper, and Melchior. This was a favorite custom of the Polish mothers of the East Hammond Community, and, needless to say, in anticipation of this visit, the house was spotless. The little food set aside for his visit was seldom eaten, for Fr. Szezukowski was usually in a hurry to get to the next house. Thus, a light dessert was enjoyed after he left by the family gathered for the occasion.

These post Christmas events, however, were only a temporary joyful reprieve from the constant concern most were experiencing during these dark days of the depression. The last really wholesome meal that most could remember was Christmas Wigilia.

Shortly after the beginning of the new year, the East Hammond community became aware of a new government program titled the Civil Conservation Corps (CCC camps). They further discovered that their single young men, ages 17 to 27, were eligible to participate. They understood that the young men would earn as much as $1.00 a day and that 25 of these dollars would be sent home monthly by the government to assist their families. Of keenest interest to young men like the Yellow Jackets was that, in addition to the pay, they would be fed and housed at government expense.

Kal Borbely came running down the street to where Lefty was standing in front of his house, "Are you and Walt going?"

Laughing, Lefty said, "you got to be kiddin', Kal. They don't know what they're in for. They'll have to bring in extra food trucks at these camps just for the Yellow Jackets."

Kal agreed and said, "I'm gettin' hungry just thinkin' about it."

Very soon most of the Yellow Jackets had been approved and found themselves in southern Indiana at various state parks where over the months they were there, they ate, ate, ate, worked, and thrived. For many Yellow Jackets it was the first time they had heard a southern accent. And for young men from Bedford, Boonville, Jasper, and Tell City, they had never known so many Poles who could actually converse in their foreign language.

Lefty found that he enjoyed grits, and particularly biscuits and gravy which he continued to be fond of into his 90s. The Yellow Jackets relocated large trees, built roads and trails, picnic tables, and fireplaces. They worked long days and enjoyed the comraderie of young men they would never have known, and they often talked of these special days the rest of their lives.

CCC Camps, Lefty on right

Hitting the Rails

When the Yellow Jackets returned home from the CCC camps, they returned to a very hot summer and a community still struggling with the basics—food being at the top of the list. Therefore, a number of Yellow Jackets, including Lefty and Walt, hit the rails to see some portion of this great country and to relieve the family table of one more mouth to feed. They were, in their terms, "going on the bum." Lefty and Walt both headed east, but separately, Walt leaving a week before Lefty. Both left with different intended agendas.

The first train that Lefty boarded was coming through Chicago, through East Hammond, heading for points east. He jumped the train in late evening. His heart was pounding, and the adrenaline flowing. He could not sleep, so he strapped himself to the top of the boxcar and used his jacket as a pillow under his head. He listened mile after mile to the sound of the train wheels as they created their own melody moving across the tracks. Mile after mile, further and further from his home. The rush was overwhelming. He was young and strong and took pleasure in knowing that he was incapable of predicting the next day or the days after. It would be a true adventure. As he lay there in the late summer night warmth, it got darker than any night that he had ever experienced. The number of stars in the sky exceeded anything he could have ever imagined. The shooting stars, both overhead and from the corners of the sky, took his breath away. He had been gone from home only a brief time, yet in this brief time he knew he would never be the same again. He had gotten closer to his God that night, and he had gotten closer to himself. He missed Walt. It would have been great to have shared this, but he knew that opportunity would come. So, he just continued to lie there, his eyes to the sky, the warm breeze running over his body, and the perpetual sound of the melody of the train wheels below him.

As early dawn came, he felt a bit cooler, so he sat up and slipped on his jacket. He noticed that the train was slowing, and though not feeling tired, he was hungry. He had brought some food with him, but he was trying to make it last. Then, for the first time he heard voices. They were coming from below him. They were coming from the inside of the boxcar. As the train continued to slow, the voices seemed to be louder. Up ahead he could see in the distance what appeared to be a fairly large station stop. Closer, he could now see what appeared to be men lined along both sides of the tracks. They appeared to have shot guns, or long hickory axe handles. His inclination was to jump from the train.

He got up and was preparing to climb down to a point where he could jump when he ran into one of the men from inside the boxcar coming up. The older man, sensing immediately Lefty's concern, looked at him and said, "Sit down, kid. It's gonna be okay."

Then the man stood up on the slowly moving boxcar. As Lefty looked front and back, he could see other men climbing to the tops of other boxcars. Before long, there must have been 70 to 80 men, all standing on what appeared to be no less than 70 boxcars. He could still hear talking from within the boxcar now sounding like many men. The train stopped. Lefty looked at the sign on the station. It said, "CONNEAUT," in large letters with smaller letters below that spelled, "Ohio."

Four or five of the men on the ground, carrying what were now clearly long wooden clubs, stepped forward. One of the biggest yelled to the men on the train, "You are trespassing on private property. You have five minutes to get off of this train and peacefully leave the area or we will remove you."

The man standing next to Lefty shouted first to the men on the train, "Don't any of you men move. Stay right where you are on this train."

Then to the men on the ground he shouted, "We are a train of American Veterans from World War I. Some of us fought as comrades with some of your fallen fathers and uncles. We are on our way again to Washington to demand our bonuses that were promised to us."

It was quiet and all one could hear was the sound of the stopped train engine up ahead with its rhythm of releasing steam. Then a very unusual thing happened. The big man on the ground who had spoken directing the men to leave the train, without saying a word, dropped his club, stepped back several paces and then raised his right hand to his forehead in military salute and kept it there. The men both on the boxcars and within raised their right hands and in military fashion returned the salute. Simultaneously, other men on the ground were discarding their clubs, stepping back, and also saluting. The train began to slowly move and as it pulled from the Conneaut station, several men on the ground and a number on the train waved to one another as they passed.

The vet looked down at Lefty and said, "C'mon, kid. You can't stay up here. There's a storm coming."

Lefty followed him down and into the boxcar.

When he got into the boxcar, he found the car to be fairly full with about 15 men. The man who brought him down motioned to a man across the car and said, "Hey, Mickey, you guys make a little space there for the kid," and to Lefty he said, "Where you from, kid? Where you goin'? Were you on top of the car all night?"

Lefty wasn't sure which question to answer first. Over the next 45 minutes to an hour, they shot the bull about many things, including football, their concerns regarding Roosevelt's veto of the bill to provide the bonus, where they were from, and cautions to a young guy alone, hitting the rails. After awhile, the predicted storm came with its light rain against the outside of the boxcar. The sound of the train wheels and the rain made Lefty sleep.

"Hey, kid, think this is your stop. Said you wanted to go to Niagara Falls and this is as close as this train will get ya to it."

Lefty, waking from his sleep, responded, "Thanks, Mickey."

The train had slowed sufficiently to where someone could jump off. He looked around and then said, "Thanks, guys."

This brought about a number of responses:

"Take care, kid."

"Don't take any wooden nickels."

"Watch your ass, kid."

Lefty jumped. It was midday and he was tired and hungry. He had finished his food, but was still hungry. He began walking and within an hour came to a small town. It was nearing 4:00 p.m., and it was Saturday. Near the edge of the town he came upon an old fruit market/store. He took a chance and went in. The owner was closing. Lefty looked at him and said, "Sir?"

The owner just peered over his glasses. "Sir, do you have any old food that might rot and you'll have to throw it away?"

The owner continued to peer over his glasses, looking at Lefty and then smiled. "Come here, kid."

He led Lefty to a shed at the back of the store, handed him a broom and said, "Clean this place up really good in the next 20 minutes. I need to lock up real soon. You do a good job and we'll look around for something that's rotting." Then he smiled.

Twenty minutes later the owner came to the shed area with a big paper bag filled with no less than 15 old and very ripe bananas. He gave the bag to Lefty and said to him, "You stay out of trouble now, don't steal, ask to work always before you ask for food. Don't get arrested. Now, go. Eat your bananas."

Lefty thanked him and then continued his walk. He was now out of town and nearing a huge billboard some ten yards or so off the road. Weeds were growing everywhere. He found a place to sit, leaning up against one of the 6 x 6 inch posts holding up the billboard and began to eat. He didn't think he had ever had any food that tasted so good. He ate twelve of the fifteen bananas and though he could have eaten all of them, he decided to save a few for later. It was getting dark now.

There was a soft breeze. He wasn't hungry and he fell asleep.

"Hey, kid. Wake up. You can't sleep out here. It's illegal."

Lefty opened his eyes, then put his left hand before his face. Whoever woke him and was talking to him had a bright light flashing in his eyes.

"You hear me, kid? It's illegal."

It was a cop. Lefty responded, "Yes, sir," and got to his feet.

The officer said, "What you got in the bag?"

"Bananas."

"Where you goin', kid?"

Lefty looked at him and said, "Sir, I'd really like to get to the Niagara Falls. I've heard they're beautiful, and I'd really like to see them."

The Officer paused for a moment and then said, "Follow me."

He then took Lefty to his squad car and had him get into the front seat. Then the officer got in and said, "You got about 16 miles, kid. I'm gonna drive ya eight to a road that you'll need to walk to get there. It's 3:00 a.m. right now. I figure you'll get there sometime around dawn. You'll hear 'em long before you see 'em, but when you finally do see 'em, you won't want to stop looking at 'em. They'll take your breath away. That's what they did to me when I first saw 'em some 20 years ago when I was about your age. I'm dropping you off now at the same road I walked."

Lefty just looked at him and said, "Thanks, sir. Thanks a lot."

The officer replied, "Wish for a moment I could go back in time, kid, and walk it with ya. They somehow never sound and look quite as awesome as that first time you walk up to 'em. Good luck, kid."

Lefty got to his Niagara Falls that early summer morning and they were all he had imagined and been told and more. He stood there the whole day. Then he made the promise that so many Depression kids made to themselves. Some day if he was blessed with his own family, he would bring them here. Some day he would bring them here and he would show them this. And like so many other Depression youth who had made such promises, he did. He did bring them there, and they stood where he stood in awe so many years before.

New York City and the Way Home

It took Lefty a good week to work his way from Niagara Falls to New York City. He was occasionally able to work for a meal and sometimes it was simply just given to him. He walked a great deal, hitched rides where he could, and found several bum camps where once in awhile he got coffee and often got advice. Some of the advice was worth while, some was not. All of the advice was, however, well-intentioned. One piece of advice ended up being of particular importance to him and dealt with several missions in New York City. At one bum camp, it was noted that his shoes were useless and probably hurting his feet. The observer was correct. He was told that if he worked for one of the missions doing dishes or cleaning etc., he could get a cot, meals, and earn enough for a shoe voucher So he hit the rails again and was off to New York City.

Lefty had seen big cities. Chicago was near home and he had been there several times. He and Kal Borbely had skipped Coach Huffine's football practice once in the fall of 1933 to go to the Chicago World's Fair. He had attended football games at the University of Chicago where he saw Jay Berwanger play. But nothing could have prepared him for the city of New York. Every other city experience he had had to that point in his life was not a valid comparison to what New York did to the word "city." Where Chicago had several big sky scrapers, New York City had a hundred. Where Chicago had streets with traffic, New York streets were an unending circus of cars, trucks, trolleys, buses, police on foot and horseback, and an endless array of wheeled vehicles moving products and people in and out and endless colors and sounds coming at you from every corner of your perceptual experience. For Lefty, New York City was like the circus experience his mother had taken him to when he was four years old. He remembered that he cried because he was overwhelmed with all that was bombarding his senses and he simply couldn't take it all in.

He finally found the mission and went in, and that was good for it was relatively quiet in there.

"Young man, what can I do for you?" asked a rather handsome, middle-aged woman wearing a conservative, yet fashionable dress and sounding as though she had something to do with running this place.

Lefty pulled his cap into his hands and responded, "Ma'am, I'm looking for work and a place to stay."

The woman smiled, looked him over and said, "Work we can give you as well as a cot upon which to sleep and food to nourish your body. What we can also give you is an opportunity to nourish your soul though this last we shall not force upon you, for if this last is to be meaningful nourishment, it must come from you. Is this agreeable, young man?"

Lefty said still with his hat in hand, "Yes, Ma'am."

Then she replied, "And your name would be?"

"Lefty Golarz."

She then explained, "No, I meant your given name."

Lefty was caught off guard. "John, uh, John."

"Then follow me, John. I am Sarah."

The experience of the mission was, for Lefty, a great reprieve from the wanderings of the past three weeks. He had a cot, got three light meals each day, worked from 6:00 a.m. to 2:00 p.m., and had time each afternoon to reach out into New York City and visit something he had always wanted to see. So, he went to see the Statue of Liberty and Ellis Island, stood at the base and walked around the Empire State Building several times since he could not afford to go to the top, crossed the Brooklyn Bridge, visited the Bronx, Broadway, Times Square, and so much more. One night after he had been at the mission about ten days, he lay in his cot looking at the ceiling. He was saying quietly a short prayer that his mother had taught him to say as he went to sleep. In the next cot was an old-timer that he had often talked to named Jed.

"Say, Lefty. See you got your shoes."

"Yeah, Jed, and they really feel good."

"What's that mumbling you do each night as you go to sleep. I can't make out any of the words."

Lefty remarked, "That's because it's in Polish. My Ma taught it to me."

"You got a Ma still alive, Lefty?"

"Yeah. She's home with my Pa, sisters and kid brother."

"Lefty, you know how many guys in this room have a home with a Ma and Pa and brothers and sisters who love 'em?"

Lefty slowly responded, "No, Jed, I guess I never thought of it."

"None of 'em, kid. None of 'em."

Then he continued, "You know, when you're out here like you are, a hundred, no a thousand things could go wrong. So far for you, it ain't happened. Maybe it's the little prayer you say each night, I don't know. I ain't one for givin' advice. Lord knows, there's not a lot in my life to be proud of. But, if you don't mind..."

Lefty interrupted, "Go ahead, Jed."

"I see a brand new pair of shoes under your bed just achin' to go home to a family that loves you. So, before one of those thousand things that can go wrong does go wrong, go home, kid. Go home."

The next morning Lefty laced his new shoes, grabbed all of his things, and went to breakfast with Jed. They sat there across the table from one another, not really saying anything, just eating their eggs. When Lefty finished, he looked up at Jed and said, "Gonna miss you, old-timer."

"Gonna miss you too, kid. Lefty, this fall, after you win your last football game, if you don't mind, drop me a line and tell me about it. If I ain't here, they'll know where to find me. I ain't goin' too far."

Lefty started to say something, "Well…"

Jed interrupted him, "Just go now, kid…just go."

Lefty smiled and nodded, threw his jacket over his shoulder, turned and left. Jed just sat there and watched him go.

The train ride to Buffalo that night was cold, and all the boxcars he tried had been locked, so he belted himself on a metal ladder between two boxcars. He'd be out of the wind that ran across the tops of cars, but sleeping would be difficult. The miles ran by and he grew wearier. He asked himself, "If I fall asleep, will I fall off? Will I possibly fall between the cars onto the tracks?" Then he decided, "better stay awake—just doze."

But he was just too tired. "Can't doze, or I'll fall asleep."

He considered jumping off the train and finding a place to sleep in the tall grasses and weeds along the railroad property, but the train was going too fast. He then decided to just hang on, hang on and pray he could stay awake. Then the unexpected.... the train began to slow. It was slowing enough for him to get off. He unstrapped, lowered himself, and slid off onto the rocks that make up the bed for the tracks. He was stiff, but able to walk. As he glanced at his train slowly passing him, he saw out of the corner of his eye an open boxcar. He ran, caught it, and jumped aboard. It looked safe. There was no one inside, and he could sit, even lay down, maybe sleep, maybe sleep all the way to Buffalo.

Good fortune was on his side. The train shuddered and it woke him up. He was in Buffalo and he had gotten there safely. He left his train and found he was on the outskirts of a roundhouse area. So, he began searching for a train heading west toward Chicago. He was walking westward on tracks which he was sure would eventually have westbound trains.

Up ahead, coming toward him on the tracks, were two guys. As he got nearer, he could sense that they were trouble. It wasn't anything they did, particularly. Just a sense. Both looked a bit bigger than he was and a bit older. As they approached to about ten yards, one yelled out, "Hey, how you doin', kid?"

He now noticed that this guy had a thick, dowel-shaped piece of wood about a foot long in his left hand. As they came even nearer, the two spread apart so as to provide him a way to walk between them. He was scared. He really couldn't turn and run. That wasn't where he needed to go, and anyway, it was too late. He was really close now and their movements made it clear that they intended to surround him. He then smiled at them, raised his left hand in the manner of a wave, and before he brought his hand down, he clenched his left fist, took a quick step to the guy with the stick and decked him with a solid left-cross to his jaw. The guy dropped straight down. Then as quickly as he could turn, he swung at the other guy who was now attempting to back peddle. He caught him in the chest. The guy went down to his knees, and Lefty ran.

He ran down those tracks as fast as he could. He ran and ran and didn't slow down for about a mile and a half. Only then did he look back. For as far back as he could see, the tracks were clear and coming his way, going west, was a train, probably coming from the roundhouse. As it neared him, he could see that it was picking up speed but wasn't yet too fast to jump on. The day was warm and sunny, so no need to find an open car. He would board and head for the top. He was still looking over his shoulder as he strapped himself on top of the boxcar. He couldn't relax after what he had just experienced. So, he just sat up there and watched the trees go by and, eventually, the southeastern end of Lake Erie came into view. It had the look of Lake Michigan, his own lake, and then a wave of homesickness washed over him.

He was hungry now, really hungry. He knew that Conneaut, Ohio would be his next stop. You learn some things ridin' the rails. He also remembered being told in one of the New York bum camps that he might get a sandwich in Conneaut a couple of houses down from the convent near the tracks, a Mrs. Simons or Simpson—bunch a little kids. On the bum you remember the things that might get you a meal. The train was now slowing and he could see up ahead what looked like the Conneaut station. He had been there, of course, a month ago with the WWI Vets. Had it been only a month? It seemed so, so much longer. It seemed like months, or maybe a year. So much had happened. So many places. So many people. So many experiences. And he was no longer the person who left his home. He was different somehow. Different in lots of ways but he wasn't yet sure how. It would take him awhile to figure this all out. Maybe quite awhile.

The station was now upon them and the train was nearly stopped. He got off. He was now being driven purely by hunger. It was not difficult to find the convent for there were two nuns in the backyard, not the habit of his St. Mary's nuns, but clearly Catholic nuns. He came across the open area and walked slowly and directly toward the sisters who had by this time looked up and were watching him come toward them.

As he neared them, he removed his cap, clasped it in his hands, and said, "Hello, sisters."

Each nun responded, "Hello."

Then he said, "Sisters, my name is John Golarz, and I just got off of that train that came from Buffalo."

The slightly shorter of the two said, "Well, John, I'm Sister Mary of the Rosary and this is Sister Eulalia, and what might we do for you, John?"

"Well, sisters, I was told that living near you is a Mrs. Simons or Simpson, and that if I knocked at her back…."

Sister Eulalia interrupted and said, "You're hungry, aren't you, John?"

Lefty nodded.

Then Sister Eulalia said, "It's Mrs. Simpson, John," and then she pointed to the house and continued, "She hasn't much, John, other than a growing family, but if she can, she will likely give you a sandwich. She is, John, a true woman of grace, so you go there now—you're hungry."

Lefty thanked them and made the short trip to the Simpson back door. Two little boys were playing in the backyard. He knocked on the door. It opened and through the broken screen door, he could see a woman in a house dress and apron, some thirty years old. An attractive, yet obviously hard-working woman who looked out at him, and said, "Yes, young man?"

"Ma'am, my name is John, and I just got off that train and I'm really hungry and…"

She stopped him and replied, "John, we don't have much, but I think I can give you a sandwich. You just sit there on that step and wait a moment. I'll be right back."

Lefty sat there watching the boys play in the yard. He couldn't have had any idea that the woman preparing his sandwich in the kitchen of that house on Madison Street, would, five years later, in 1940, have a daughter that she and her husband, Michael Simpson, would name Marion, or further that this child would years later become the beloved wife of his oldest son Raymond, the author of this book.

It was approaching evening now and though the sandwich did not fill him, it did sustain. He was now looking for a train going west. It was a night much like the night he left home. Soon, he lay strapped to the top of the boxcar with his jacket propped under his head as a pillow. The night was again that very, very dark night, and the train wheels created their melody with the tracks. The breeze ran across and caressed his body as he watched the shooting stars cut slices through the sky.

The bum had been much more than the experience he had anticipated and like so many of the other Depression men of his age, he would talk of it the rest of his life. But right now, it was just a time to look up into the sky, perhaps doze, and soon be home.

Amateur vs. Pro

The Yellow Jackets were home. It had been a long spring and summer that included the CCC camps and the individual bums taken by so many. Mothers and Fathers, kid sisters and brothers, friends and other relatives, old men, Wusic, Fatty Grisha, Johnny Long and a host of others who made up the East Hammond community were very happy to see these yellow-sweatered, young warriors back walking their streets. A common remark made to them, however, as they encountered some community old-timers who had not seen them for some time was, "Vat happen you?" "Loose tuh much veight." "Beh tuh skinneh."

The Yellow Jackets who had come back from extensive bums were on average 15 pounds lighter than when they had left. They weren't overweight when they left, but now their appearance was akin to a veteran wrestler who mid-season drops weight to compete in a lighter class. What came home from the bums was a healthy, injury-free, leaner, and much faster Yellow Jacket Football team.

The Yellow Jackets wasted no time. Though their first scheduled game arranged by the new Calumet League would not be until October 20th against Hammond Motor Express at Turner Field, they were itching to get started and their fans were anxious to watch them. Therefore, beginning in late August they initiated their three to four day a week practice schedule at their field. At each practice there were often about 100 people of all ages in attendance watching their Yellow Jackets.

These days of 1935 were exciting days for post high school football. Professional teams were forming and working feverishly to attract the best players coming out of college. Professional compensation was still low. Therefore, many of the best college players who had completed college would matriculate into professions for which they had prepared. Oh, they would be available for a post graduation charity game or two, but a permanent spot on some emerging pro team was not of interest. The pro teams, looking for national press, would and did, therefore, make themselves available for such charity games.

In these mid-thirties, there was also occurring annually a nationally prominent football game that pitted the college all stars of that year against the best team in the fledgling National Football League. The first of such games was played in 1934 at Chicago's Soldier Field in front of 78,000 fans. The game was between the College All Stars and the Chicago Bears and resulted in a scoreless tie. Then came the 1935 College All Stars, considered a truly exceptional and talented class. They were 41 in total number and had 14 players from the powerful Big Ten as well as four from Notre Dame. They also had strong representation from Alabama, favored to again play in the Rose Bowl and win the national championship. According to newspapers of that day, the primary purpose of the All Star vs. Bears game was to judge whether amateur or professional football was supreme. The odds that year of 1935 were heavily in favor of the College All Stars. Yet, on August 29th again in Soldier's Field the score was Bears 5, All Stars 0. Something was happening to professional football.

The Yellow Jackets were playing a sport receiving more national, broad regional, and local attention. And before this 1935 season would be over the attention the Yellow Jackets would receive would be more than they or their fans could have anticipated. They would not gain national attention, but in their own circles of competition and broader circles, they would be known and respected.

Meanwhile, the hottest item in football that September in the northwest corner of Indiana was not the newly formed football league or Yellow Jacket football. Rather, it was the game that would be played at the East Chicago Roosevelt football field between the Chicago Bears and the Gillies All Stars. The game would take place on Wednesday, September 11th, under the lights. A crowd of twelve to fifteen thousand was expected and additional bleachers had been erected to accommodate this larger crowd. The Gillies All Stars were not from Lake County. Their coach, Fred Gillies, was more of an event recruiter than a football coach. So, with a great deal of financial backing from local power brokers, he would recruit from across the nation. He would recruit only former great college stars who had not gone into the pros. He had a reputation for being successful at this and the teams he recruited had, to this point in the evolution of professional football, competed very well against the best professional teams in the world. But the glory days of Fred Gillies were waning. The professional teams were getting better. They were becoming more successful at recruiting. They had secured some of the greatest running backs and linemen to have played the game of college football. Most importantly, the players going into the pros were staying longer and beginning to play in a manner that reflected their growing knowledge of the skills and styles of each other. They were becoming teams, not simply groups of highly talented individuals.

Thus, the final score of the September 11, 1935 charity game seen by some 15,000 fans in East Chicago, was Chicago Bears 40, Gillies All Stars 0. There was a change in the air. It would take years to mature, but a new level of football was coming.

Advantage—Speed

"Kick another one out here, Lefty. You must be getting 65 yards on these punts."

"Okay, Kal. Get ready for this one, I can feel a 70 yarder coming."

Lefty punted the ball, a booming high spiral that just seemed to hang up there and float down gently to Kal Borbely.

"67 yards, yells Kal."

"Ah, bullshit, Kal. That was 70."

"Look, Lefty, when it's 70, I'll tell you it's 70. When it's 67, I'll tell you it's 67. Don't want me lyin' to you, do you?"

"Nah. You just tell it like it is, Kal. C'mon, we better get over to Wusic's. Don't want to be late for the team meeting."

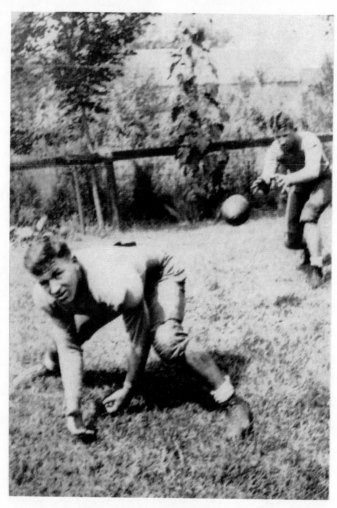

Kal and Lefty

They grabbed their football and began the short walk from their field, across Columbia Avenue to Wusic's gas station. It had been a beautiful fall day. The neighborhood trees were in full color and the air had a crisp, clean smell that seems so characteristic of late October when the temperature in late afternoon hovers around 50 degrees. Some neighborhood old-timers were already burning leaves and that aroma, stirred into the crisp fall air, created a smell that one never seems to forget. So, Lefty and Kal took a deep breath. It was time for a football game.

"Everybody here?" Fatty asked Walt.

"All here, Fatty."

Fatty began to address the team.

"Well, guys, tomorrow is what we have been practicing and preparing for. The game tomorrow is at 2:00 p.m. at Turner Field on the north side of Hammond, so be here at 1:00 p.m. You all know it's not a long ride. Maybe ten minutes or so and that will give us some time to warm up. Don't underestimate Motor Express. They have some of the best football talent in this area including Chicago. They're not coming tomorrow to pass the time. They intend to beat us.

"We'll be doing some things differently than we did last year. We are much faster and we are deeper at every position than we have ever been. So, even though some of you might think you should play till you're dog-tired like you often did last year, our pre-season plan is to avoid that. Our plan is to take advantage of our depth. You've heard this now in all of our practices. We are fast. We're healthy and probably in the best physical condition we've ever been in. So, during the game we rotate players. We rotate. We rotate. And we rotate. When you're in there, hit 'em as hard as you can and pursue each play till the whistle. Pursue. Pursue. Pursue. Mike Wusic and I have scouted all of our league opponents and we're here to tell you that usually you will find that they are a little bigger than we are, but nobody's faster. So, when you're in there, hit 'em hard and pursue. Then you'll come out and rest. After you're rested you go back in. Hit 'em hard again and pursue. Then out again and rest. Even though you don't think you're tired, you rest. By the second quarter, no later than the third, they will belong to us.

Pulkowski, Fyda, Topolski, Malakovich, Milobar, you understand?"

They each nodded without saying a word.

Fatty continued.

"On defense we never let 'em out of their backfield. Remember, our advantage is speed and depth. A tackle for loss is what we expect on each play. If they make it to or past the line of scrimmage, get your ass outta there, and get someone fresh in your place. You're not gettin' the job done. We get first downs, they don't. We score touchdowns, they don't. We win, they don't.

Anybody have any questions?"

There's a long silence in the Yellow Jacket room. Then Walt said, "See all you guys here tomorrow at 1:00 p.m."

Season Opener—A Rout

The Yellow Jackets won the toss and elected to kick off. As expected, Walt kicked the ball into the end zone and Hammond Motor Express took the ball on the 20 yard line. The first three plays were a disaster for Motor Express. On first down, their big fullback was hit and downed by nose guard Malakovich as he was taking the handoff. On the second play, their right halfback, having just taken a pitch from their quarterback, was hit four yards behind the line of scrimmage by Tony Hayduk and Alex Fyda. Third down, Hammond Motor Express found themselves needing 15 yards for a first down. Their quarterback took the snap, dropped back, and as he turned to locate a receiver and throw, he was hit simultaneously by Novalik and Lefty who had both blitzed. It was fourth and 18 on the 12 yard line. Motor Express was stunned and called a time out. Fatty came out to the Yellow Jacket huddle. He brought with him Walt, Kal Borbely, Mike Dotlich and Pulkowski.

In the huddle, Walt said, "Okay. Alex, Tony, Gorski and Novalik, you guys go take a breather. We have a punt to block."

Moments later, a shocked opponent saw a blocked punt, and the Yellow Jackets recovering the ball on the four yard line. Just as quickly on the following play, the Yellow Jackets first play from scrimmage, Walt, as a consequence of great offensive line blocking by Kal Borbely, ran it in over their left guard, untouched. The extra point was made and the score was Yellow Jackets 7, Motor Express 0. The crowd of nearly 900, most of whom had walked from East Hammond, were ecstatic. They had been looking forward to this game all summer, and they could not be more pleased with this reward. Their Yellow Jackets looked quick, sharp, and hungry. It was still very early in the game, but the air around the huddled Yellow Jackets was filled with confidence, and everyone there at Turner Field that afternoon could smell it.

The remainder of the game was much like the beginning. Hammond Motor Express never recovered and, despite the fact of their very talented players, the afternoon belonged to the Yellow Jackets. Whether Hammond Motor Express tried to run up the middle, around end, or off tackle, they were met with ferocious tackling, either at the line or before they could get out of the backfield. Pulkowski, Hayduk, Milobar, Malakovich, Borbely and Lefty were particularly aggressive all afternoon. If the Yellow Jackets had not fumbled twice while attempting to score in the second half, the final score would have been much worse. As it was, the final score was Yellow Jackets 19, Hammond Motor Express 0. Hammond Motor Express converted for only one down in the entire game—the Yellow Jackets for 21. The game was a rout.

They were not at their home field, so they couldn't walk across the street and cluster in small groups in front of Wusic's. But no one who had walked from East Hammond seemed to notice. They were with their Yellow Jackets and their Yellow Jackets had won. They had won convincingly. So, the walk home could wait a moment on this fine fall, late afternoon. This was not home, but they would cluster on this field surrounding their favorite sons, nephews, neighbors, brothers or beaus, and they would not rush this moment. It was theirs to savor and savor they would with their young men, this team of Yellow Jackets.

Crown Point—A Drubbing

It was Monday night at Wusic's and a team of very happy Yellow Jackets was gathered. Soon Walt and Fatty would call for order, but for the moment it seemed best to allow, encourage and participate in the laughter, comraderie, and light horse play. It would be a long season, and Walt and Fatty understood that these moments of levity and brotherhood were the life blood of what sustains a great team. The moment continued and then, one by one, and in small groups, the team members began to settle into their favorite spots. The team had decided to start the meeting.

Fatty nodded to Walt, and then Walt started, "Guys, we had a really great game, and nobody got hurt, or had to finish playing the game with broken ribs. Then Walt and all the Yellow Jackets looked at Tony Hayduk.

"Doesn't hurt when you breathe, does it Tony?"

Tony instantly replied, "No. No, Walt."

The entire team broke into laughter and a moment later Tony too. Lefty reached over and mussed his hair.

Then Walt continued, "This next week is gonna be tough. As most of you know, we have two games. The first against Crown Point on Friday night under the lights in Crown Point, and the second on Sunday, at 2:00 p.m. at Turner Field, against the Indiana Harbor Night Hawks. We had scheduled Crown Point before we knew we were going to be in this Calumet Region Football League. So, rather than cancelling you guys wanted to play 'em, so it's two games. Mike Wusic's a little concerned about drivin' the truck too fast. It's not running really well and there's Route 8 on the way into Crown Point with all those potholes. So Mike wants us in the truck and on our way Friday night by 5:30 p.m. Kick off is scheduled for 7:30 p.m. Any questions?"

Pulkowski spoke up, "Yeah. I got a question. We got any new tarps?"

Walt looked at Pulkowski and said, "Where the hell would we get money for new tarps, Pul?

Just don't sit with your ass out of one of the tarp holes."

There was much laughter in the room and Pulkowski responded, "Right, sit next to Alex and Malakovich and not have my ass stick out of one of the holes—right, Walt."

Much more laughter. Now Walt, Fatty, Pulkowski, and every team member was laughing. The Yellow Jackets were in good spirits, and new tarps or not, the trip out to Crown Point on Friday was a trip they were looking forward to making.

Soon, everyone began leaving the room. Their next stop would be Crown Point.

The following is taken from the sports section of the Hammond Times Newspaper, dated October 26, 1935, the day after the Crown Point game:

"The powerful Maywood Yellow Jacket team invaded Crown Point territory last night and administered a 19 to 0 drubbing of the local team. It was a nip and tuck affair until the last quarter, which showed Crown Point outclassed in every department of the game. The leading scorers for the Maywood Yellow Jackets were both Golarz brothers and Gorski who intercepted two passes and kicked an extra point."

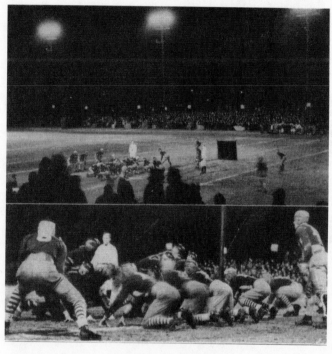

Under the lights

A Special Team Meeting

Johnny Gorski and Alex came early to the team meeting on Saturday and spotted Fatty.

"Hey, Fatty. Did you see today's paper? Mrs. Zothkiewicz at the grocery store on Kenwood clipped out the article for us. Says we're powerful and we give people drubbings. Is that like kickin' the shit out of somebody?"

Fatty responded angrily, "You guys shouldn't read that shit. It's not good for you. Just makes you overconfident, even though you don't know it. I'll tell you one thing for sure. The Night Hawks are readin' that article today too, and it's like wavin' a red flag in front of a bull's face. They're gonna come into the game pissed off. We're the guys on top of the hill now and they're gonna come to knock us off."

Gorski responded, "Yeah. You're right, Fatty. They're tough enough without pissing 'em off."

By this time the team had gathered and Fatty took the floor. "Mike wants us here tomorrow at 1:00 p.m. Kick off is, as usual, 2:00 p.m. Turner Field. Any questions?"

Joe Golec, sounding a little upset, said, "You know tomorrow we play again at Turner Field and I understand that the only home game we're gonna have all season is next week against Lansing"

Walt answered, "That's right, Joe."

"Well, I think it's bullshit. My Ma would like to come to our games and there's no way for her to get to Turner Field. She sure can't walk that far and then back."

George Stoming chimed in, "Joe's right, and a lot of us have been talkin' about this."

Walt interjected, "Well, guys, this is one of the prices you pay when you join a league."

Pulkowski added, "Well, maybe the price is too high."

The room was filled now with talk, mostly in small groups. Fatty said, "Guys, remember, we agreed to one year as a trial to this league, and if we end up not likin' it, we can go back to independent next year. Right, Walt, Lefty?"

Lefty then said, "Guys, keep a record of what you like and don't like about this league thing. If after this season, we vote not to stay, then we can go back on our own."

The players started to settle down and it got quieter in the room. Fatty then said, "Anybody got anything else before we break up?"

Walter Kwolek said, "Well, I don't know if this is the place..."

Walt interrupted, "Hey, this is always the place. Go ahead, Walter."

"Well, most of you guys know about Mr. Kopinski." In the room there were lots of acknowledgements and heads nodding, but not everyone seemed to know.

"Well, he got hurt at work, fell off a ladder while he was paintin' some 20 or 25 feet off the ground. The fall broke his back and he's paralyzed from the waist down. Looks like he's gonna be in a wheel chair the rest of his life. Guess he was workin' up there ten minutes after his shift was over, tryin' to finish the last part of the job. So, the company says they won't give him any pension or insurance coverage cause the accident took place on his own time and he had no business bein' up there."

There was a great deal of quiet grumbling and Lefty, loud enough to be heard, said, "Those bastards."

Walter continued, "Well, I guess his daughter Sarah, she's the oldest, you know. Two younger ones, but they're not in school yet. Well, Sarah, she was in St. Mary's in the eighth grade. Well, she quit school and is doin' housework out somewhere on Indi-Illi Parkway, tryin' to help the family make it. Guess it's pretty rough there for them right now."

The room was completely silent.

"Like I said. I don't know if this is the place."

Walt stopped him, "Walter, this is always the place. We're the Maywood Yellow Jackets, and we don't just play football. We're gonna think of something to do, Walter, we're gonna think of something to do. You did the right thing bringin' it here. You did the right thing."

There were lots and lots of signs of agreement. Then slowly the team began to leave. The meeting was over and the Yellow Jackets had something to think about besides tomorrow's game against their arch rivals, the Indiana Harbor Night Hawks.

Yellow Jackets vs. Night Hawks

Sunday, October 27th, game day, was a day of contrasts. Mike Wusic's truck broke down on the way to Turner Field, so the team had to get off and walk from Summer Street. The Night Hawks, on the other hand, came in a new yellow bus made available by the city government and the public schools. Pulkowski and Fyda ripped their football pants badly getting off the truck after it broke down, so they needed to wrap parts of the torn tarps around their waists until they got to the field and had someone loan them old large pants that they tied with rope at the waist and then rolled up the pant legs. Actually, their make-shift attire wasn't noticeable when they stood with the team, for the Yellow Jackets' uniforms were the oldest and least uniform in the new league. Occasionally, some politician running for office would give them new inexpensive jerseys with an ad requesting political support. But these jerseys tended to tear easily and lasted only a game or two. The oldest jersey on the team was worn by Heinie Milobar and had been given to him by Fatty Grisha. Fatty had worn it in 1923 when he played fullback for the old Hammond Boosters. To describe the specific attire of the rest of the team would take some time and simply embarrass our Yellow Jackets.

One jersey, however, because of its uniqueness, does demand description. Mike Malakovich in 1934 made the mistake of telling his mother, Mrs. Malakovich, that he really didn't have a jersey. So, as a surprise to Mike she knit him one. It was bright yellow with a big "M" in dark grey on the back. When he wore it, and he had to because his Pa went to all the home games plus Turner Field, you could pick out Mike even when it got dark. It was like watching one big yellow shirt whipping around alone on the dark field. One yellow shirt with a big "M" on the back. Of course, when she washed it, it got a little smaller. If you were an opponent across from Mike, the one thing you really never wanted to do when you got down in your stance was to look at him, then his jersey and smile or laugh. He waited for that, and if you did that, it would really piss him off. And you really didn't want to piss-off Mike Malakovich. In 1935, the Indiana Harbor Night Hawks were wearing new uniforms, a gift from the Indiana Harbor Chamber of Commerce in recognition of their participation in the newly formed Calumet Region Football League.

The third notable contrast was the size of the individual members of the teams. The Night Hawks may have had the biggest players in the league; whereas, the Yellow Jackets, if not the smallest, would certainly compete for that distinction.

The final contrast was not visible. The Night Hawks came to Turner Field that Sunday afternoon with a fine football team that would ultimately conclude the season of 1935 with several wins. But when they stepped onto that field that Sunday, they could hardly know that they had entered a lion's den, and the lions, known as the Yellow Jackets, were savage, hungry and unrelenting. By game's end, the Night Hawks would have achieved only two first downs to the Yellow Jackets 17, and the final score would be Yellow Jackets 13, Indiana Harbor 0.

After the game, the trip home down Calumet Avenue was a sight to behold. Traffic had to be stopped several times because no less than 150 to 200 of the Yellow Jacket fans walked with them back to Wusic's truck on Summer Street. Once there, in shifts of ten to twenty players plus fans, the truck was pushed back to East Hammond, all the way down Calumet, then east on Conkey, then south on Columbia and into Mike Wusic's gas station. The crowd and players then settled into their favorite clusters in and around the gas station. That night they stayed and talked and enjoyed each other's company til dark, when from a distance all that could be seen was one big yellow sweater with an M on the back, somewhat stationary, standing in his cluster of family, friends, and a very proud Pa.

The Remainder of a
Special Team Meeting

On Monday afternoon following the game, the Yellow Jackets had a brief meeting. They first decided that one-half of the money donated at their coming home game would go to the Kopinski family and the other half to Mike Wusic to fix the truck, and if he had any left over, he was to purchase a large tarp—two if he had enough money. Walter Kwolek, Kal, Lefty, and Heinie would arrange for a dance at Trinity Hall for Wednesday evening at 7:00 p.m., November 20th, after the Hessville game. All the proceeds from the dance would go to the Kopinski family. Walter Kwolek would be in charge of getting the money from the game and dance to Mr. Kopinski. And Finally, Walt and Fatty would talk to Mrs. Wisnewski who ran liquor out the side door of her candy store to have her contacts donate the liquor for the dance as a gesture of good will to the community. The business of the team meeting was complete. Fatty announced a 3:30 p.m. practice for the next afternoon, and the team slowly disbanded, some staying a little longer discussing their dance and liquor procurement assignments. Pulkowski volunteered to help Wusic pick out tarps, assuming enough money was left over from repairing the truck.

Homecoming

Saint Mary's Church fit well the nature of its poor Polish community. It was not a structure of bricks and stone, but rather a humble church of wood covered with shingle. It had a high bell tower up front, but this was also wood constructed and shingled. The window frames were arched, but plain and simple. The church was sturdy, well-built, and always clean, thus fit well the character of its parishioners.

On Sunday, game day, virtually all the catholic guys on the team, and that was just about everybody, went to 10:00 mass at St. Mary's. They all wore their Yellow Jacket sweaters and sat in a group up front near the Blessed Virgin's side altar. Father Ladislaus Szezukowski, the parish pastor, had been announcing at all the masses that one-half of all proceeds from this Yellow Jacket home game at 2:00 p.m. was being directed to the Kopinski family. He was also advising that all proceeds from a dance at Trinity Hall on the 20th were going to the family. The church would not be charging a usage fee for the hall that night.

Old Saint Mary's Church

The 10:00 mass was typically very well attended, and so after mass, outside on the sidewalks, the Yellow Jackets were surrounded by well-wishers Several of the older Busias complimented them regarding the fact that they all took communion. As usual, the Busias missed nothing.

It was 1:15 p.m., and the bus transporting the Lansing team was pulling up on the far side of the field. There was already quite a crowd, mostly from East Hammond, but it was clear that they would be only part of a larger crowd since substantial numbers were still streaming across Columbia Avenue from the neighborhood. The field looked sharp. Lefty and Kal had lined it very carefully. They seemed to enjoy that task, and all agreed that they were very good at it.

Lansing was not a very strong team. They did not have much of a running game, and their defense was lacking, particularly in the line. They had played two games thus far this season, and had lost both. The Yellow Jackets were, however, not about to underestimate the team whose community bordered Chicago Heights. The memory of underestimating Chicago Heights last season still stung a bit.

The community of East Hammond could not have had a better day for a football game. The temperature was near 50, and it was quite sunny with only a whisper of clouds in the sky. Many trees had lost a great number of their leaves, though some sporadic color remained. All in all, it was a perfect day for football.

Mr. Gorski and two other veterans of World War 1 were unraveling a cherished U.S. Flag in the northeast corner of the field. A hush fell over the crowd. Children stopped running and stood in place. All hats were being removed. Hands over chests. A crowd now focused on a waving flag. From every corner of the field you could hear the National Anthem being sung. Not loud, yet more than faint, all were singing, even those who had thick accents and imperfect English. As you observed them with their eyes and whole being focused on that corner, it was clear that despite their recency to America, this was *their* flag, *their* country, and they had come to watch *their* young men play *their* game of football.

At the conclusion of the National Anthem, a roar came from the crowd of some 2,000 spectators. Representatives of each team were now coming to the center of the field for the coin-toss. Representing the Yellow Jackets were Walter Kwolek and Lefty Golarz. Lansing won the toss and elected to receive.

It was a long, high kick by Walt that went into the end zone. But Lansing decided to run it out. This was not a good decision. George Stoming and Kal Borbely made a solid hit, stopping the ball carrier dead in his tracks on the 13 yard line. Lansing, first and ten on their 13. The next three downs were brutal for Lansing. They attempted three running plays, testing different parts of the Yellow Jacket line, but the Yellow Jackets were ferocious, and after three plays, Lansing found themselves punting from their 8 yard line. The rush on their punter was quick, so he was unable to get off a good kick. The kicked football, at no point got more than 20 feet above the ground, but it had distance going 30 yards beyond the line of scrimmage. It came down right between Enoch and Johnny Topolski. They were both surprised, hesitated, then both went for it. They collided and the ball shot straight up in the air and was intercepted by a Lansing end. Before anyone knew it, he had run 15 yards up field. Johnny Gorski got an angle on him and brought him down on the 50 yard line. Had he not, the kid was on his way with no one to stop him. In an instant the game had changed, and someone had kicked the Yellow Jackets in the gut while breathing new life into Lansing. The crowd became very silent and began to have flashes of last year's Chicago Heights nailbiter. The remainder of the first quarter and half way through the second quarter was a nip and tuck, seesaw battle with no distinct advantage being secured by either team.

Shortly before the end of the first half, the Yellow Jackets punted to Lansing, and Lansing found themselves with great field position, first and ten on the Yellow Jackets' 47 yard line. On their first play from scrimmage, their quarterback was preparing to hand off, when from the left side of the Yellow Jacket defensive line Polkowski broke through two players and hit the quarterback for a three yard loss. The crowd responded with waves of cheers. On second down, Mike Dotlich broke through and hit the quarterback who spun away and into the outstretched arms of Pulkowski who hit him savagely. The kid went down hard and lay there for awhile. He then asked his teammates for assistance to get to his feet. He was immediately directed by his bench to leave the field, and a replacement ran in. The crowd gave him a cheer and an extensive round of applause. It was third down now, and Lansing was feeling as they did at the very beginning of the game, uneasy and lacking confidence. Their feeling was warranted. The Yellow Jacket team was an aroused beast. Third down was a tackle for loss by Alex Fyda, and on fourth down, Walt blitzed and blocked the punt. The Yellow Jackets had possession of the ball with a full three minutes left in the half.

The next six plays were classic. Enock, 7 yards off tackle; Walt, 6 yards up the middle; Lefty, 5 yards off tackle; Walt, 8 yards off tackle. Borbely, Pulkowski and Fyda were making holes that you could drive a truck through. Novalik, 7 yards up the middle, and finally Lefty around left end following the blocking of Novalik into the end zone. The crowd went crazy, shouting, cheering, and simply ecstatic. This was their Yellow Jacket team. The team they had come to see. Walt converted and the score at halftime was Yellow Jackets 7, Lansing 0. There was no need for Pulkowski to fear that his mother was marching to the halftime huddle.

The second half was much like the last minutes of the first half. The Yellow Jackets simply dominated. Lansing played like a defeated team, and each game minute of the second half the Yellow

Jackets just gained more and more confidence. They could do no wrong and they knew it. As the game ended, the Yellow Jackets were in scoring position on Lansing's three yard line.. Chet Jasinski took a knee three times and the game ended. Yellow Jackets 27, Lansing 0.

Spirits were high. The Yellow Jackets had won their home game convincingly and were moving toward an undefeated season, winning now their fourth game. A fairly large crowd was gathering at Wusic's, and it was clear that talk and comraderie would continue at the gas station until dark. The Yellow Jackets seemed to look forward to their ritual gathering, particularly when they won. There was on these occasions much laughter, much reliving the excitement of certain plays, much fun simply being with people they knew and cared for. And so the hour got late and no one noticed. There would not be another home game this year, and they knew it. So, on this special evening they would squeeze out all the joy that the evening had to offer. They would eventually walk to their homes and not notice that they were hungry. On such nights they were full on a meal of the really important things: companionship, satisfaction with a job well-done, and the love of family and friends.

Hessville

Wusic's truck was fixed. The half time pass of the hat at the Lansing home game netted $1,025,20. Half of that, $512.60 would go to the Kopinski fund and the remainder for Wusic's truck repair, two large new tarps plus $150.00 for the Yellow Jacket Emergency Fund which to that point had never had money in it. The drive to Hessville was comfortable, judging by the smiles on the faces of Pulkowski, Fyda, and Mike Dotlich. Mike Dotlich wasn't as tall as his linemen teammates, but he weighed about the same. In stature he resembled a fire hydrant and was equally as difficult to move. In later years he would work in the same department as Lefty at Inland Steel. But for the moment, his seat on the truck was normally with Pulkowski, Fyda, and Malakovich. The drive that Sunday took about twenty minutes. South on Columbia to 173rd Street, then east on 173rd past Wicker and on to Kennedy Avenue. The park where the game would be played was large, some twenty acres and bordered by homes on two sides.

Hessville had not had a team very long, but they were doing quite well in the new league. They had a very big team but lacked speed. Nonetheless, to this point in the season they had beaten Hammond Motor Express and Lansing and had tied East Chicago. The Yellow Jackets had four wins, but only three in the new league. So, the winner of today's game would be in first place in the league. Fans in Hessville understood this, so a crowd of some 700 were on hand at game time.

Hessville kicked off and the kick was exceptional, going seven or eight yards beyond the end zone. Unfortunately, that was the extent of their exceptional play for the remainder of the afternoon. The Yellow Jackets took the ball on the twenty yard line and went into their powerful and unrelenting classic mode: Enock, up the middle for five yards; Walt, off tackle for six yards; Walt, up the middle for four yards; Novalik, off tackle for seven yards; Lefty, up the middle....They never passed. They just made holes in Hessville's defense all afternoon. In the end, the Hessville team, particularly their defense, was exhausted. This East Hammond team with enough great players to rotate players both in the backfield and on the offensive line, was unlike any team they had ever played. The final score was Yellow Jackets 28, Hessville 0. This little giant from East Hammond called the Yellow Jackets would soon be noticed and talked about beyond their immediate circle of competition.

A Dance to Remember

Normally the price of a ticket for a dance put on by the Yellow jackets at Trinity Hall was 25 cents for ladies, and 35 cents for gents. But tonight, Wednesday, November 13th, was different. Anyone attending tonight was being asked to donate 40 cents.

Trinity Hall was a fairly good-sized hall. This two-story brick structure was some 50 feet by 70 feet at its base. It was located kitty-corner from the OK Bakery in the heart of the East Hammond Community. On the main level as you came in, there was a cloak room on the left, and on the right was a bar. Directly in front, beyond the large dance floor was the stage, some four feet above the dance floor level. Most of the East Hammond children were familiar with the hall for the nuns at St. Mary's routinely had second and third graders perform on stage. These performances were usually before packed houses of parents, aunts, uncles, and grandparents. The performances focused upon the skills of children with their Polish language, normally a prepared speech, memorized poem or a prayer. Therefore, most attending the dance tonight had been to Trinity Hall many times before.

Walter, Kal, Lefty, and Heinie, knowing that tonight's affair would bring a fair number of old-timers and their wives, placed tables and chairs all around the dance floor so that there were sufficient places to sit and also observe the dance activities. Tonight's liquor (beer only) had been donated by the "friends" of Mrs. Wisnewski (70 cases). Walt and Fatty had decided that there would be a limit on consumption—three beers. They enrolled the assistance of Pulkowski, Dotlich, Fyda, and Malakovich to oversee adherence to the compliance standard.

The band was "Happy" Joe Donovan's Blue Ridge Syncopators. The Yellow Jackets had used them before and they were popular with the young people of East Hammond. In addition, they were great at polkas and were coming tonight for free. The band this night came early and were playing as people were arriving, so the festivities were underway early. Every other tune was a polka, so the chairs placed in the hall by Lefty Heinie, Kal, and Walter were getting less attention from the old-timers then had been anticipated. The evening had turned into a community affair somewhat unparalled in recent memory.

Old man Pulkowski, Wleklinski, and Golarz broke the three limit consumption rule early, and there wasn't a damn thing the appointed compliance squad could do except join in. By 9:30 the beer was gone. But it didn't matter. They just kept dancing. Around 11:00 p.m., things began to wind down and Fatty, Walt, and other Yellow Jackets were being complimented by a lot of old-timers wanting to know when the next dance was going to be. The Kopinski dance had been a success and would long be remembered.

At 10:00 a.m. the next morning at Wusic's there was a team meeting during which all the money from the dance and game earmarked for the Kopinski family was given to Walter, Tony Hayduk, and Kal Borbely to take to Mr. and Mrs. Kopinski—a total of $672.60. An additional gift of $90.00 was to be delivered by the young men on behalf of the St. Mary's Ladies' Rosary and Sacred Heart Society and the Polish Women's Polki organization, given with the condition that Sarah return to finish eighth grade at St. Mary's. At 11:00 a.m. at the Kopinski residence on Ames Avenue, Walter handed the gift to Mr. Kopinski in his wheel chair. He took it, thanked them, and wept. Kal gave the conditional gift from the St. Mary's women's organizations to Mrs. Kopinski. In that envelope with the $90.00 was an additional $150.00—the Yellow Jacket emergency fund, for as Walt, Fatty, and the rest of the Yellow Jackets concurred, "What the hell is an emergency fund for anyway?"

An Honorable and
Worthy Opponent

It was Sunday afternoon, November 17th. Today the Yellow Jackets would play their last league game of the season against the East Chicago Blue Eagles. The record of the East Chicago Blue Eagles was two wins and two ties. They, as yet, had not lost. The game would be played at Turner Field at 2:00 p.m. If the Yellow Jackets won the game, they would be the undisputed champion of the Calumet Region Football League. They would, as a consequence, be invited to play on Sunday, December 1st the Hegewisch football team, champion of the Chicago Grid League. Needless to say, Fatty's primary concern on this day was keeping the Yellow Jackets focused upon the game at hand. They would play an opponent today capable of beating them. The Blue Eagles were second in league speed only to the Yellow Jackets, but they were bigger than the Yellow Jackets, especially in the line. If East Chicago came prepared to play, and there was no reason why they wouldn't, it would be quite a game. The weather, unfortunately, was not favorable for fans from East Hammond who usually walked the two and one-half miles to Turner Field. It was windy, with snow flurries, and the temperature was not expected to climb above 25 degrees.

The game plan for the day would be as it had been for most of the season—rotate, rotate, and rotate. This team today would require that the Yellow Jackets remain fresh and strong all four quarters or they could lose. The ride over to Turner Field was again a happy ride for Pulkowski, Fyda, and the other clustered linemen. New tarps without holes were truly appreciated, especially with temperatures in the mid-20s.

At 2:00 p.m., Johnny Gorski kicked off. Walt had a sore kicking leg. The kick was a good one, and the Blue Eagles took the ball on the 20. The entire first half was, for the ultimate football fan, a great game. Both teams executed well, blocked well, and tackled well. The game was hard-hitting and fast. Those who went up to catch a pass did so at their own risk, for on both teams the defenders were ready and hit with a vengeance. The entire first half was a treasure of great, clean, skilled sportsmanlike football. For the true football fan, in a sense, it was a shame that someone might win. But someone would break the stalemate and there would be a winner.

As the second half began, the Blue Eagles kicked off. A great kick to Lefty Golarz who fielded it on the 5 yard line. Then with great downfield blocking by Golec, Milobar, and Tony Hayduk, Lefty took it 95 yards and in for the score. The stalemate had been broken. The extra point was missed, and the score was Yellow Jackets 6 and the East Chicago Blue Eagles 0.

The Blue Eagles came back strong, marching sixty yards on their next drive to the Yellow Jackets 20 yard line, three and four yards at a crack. They were, however, now tired, very tired. Walt looked them over as they huddled, then yelled to the Yellow Jacket sideline, "rotate." Seven of the eleven defensive Yellow Jacket players ran off the field and were replaced by Dotlich, Malakovich, Kwolek, Juscik, Enoch, Lefty, and Johnny Topolski, all of whom had not seen any defensive play in this second half. The series of plays that followed resulted in two tackles for loss, and the Blue Eagles turning the ball over to the Yellow Jackets after four downs. The Yellow Jackets took over on the Blue Eagles 27 yard line. The fight was going out of an honorable and worthy opponent. The Yellow Jackets, now in possession of the ball, completed the third quarter and began the fourth by marching five and six yards at a crack down the field all the way to the six yard line where Walt thrust the final dagger into the Blue Eagles heart. The extra point was kicked by Johnny Gorski, and the score was Yellow Jackets 13, Blue Eagles 0. No further scoring occurred in the game.

The nearly 700 Yellow Jacket fans who had made the trek to Turner Field that day mingled with their team for a bit and then began the walk back home. Their Yellow Jackets were the undefeated, unscored upon champions of the Calumet Region Football League. That night Lefty wrote a short letter to an old friend in a mission in New York City. He mailed it the next morning.

Next stop Hegewisch.

Rare Team Picture: Yellow Jackets 1935-1936

Smacking Hegewisch

On Sunday, December 1st, the truck trip to Turner Field was quiet. It was a cold day, much like the weather experienced for the East Chicago game, but with more snow. Wusic was actually driving rather carefully as he proceeded north on Calumet, for the road was snow packed and slippery. As he approached, the field looked different with the addition of the temporary stands now providing a seating capacity of nearly eight thousand. The anticipated crowd for the game was four thousand. The temporary additional seating was actually being done in preparation for next Sunday's game, scheduled to be between the powerful Payne Boosters and the winner of today's game. By next Sunday, there would be seating for 15,000 fans.

Hegewisch was a very powerful and successful team. They boasted of any number of players who had had highly successful football college careers but who had decided not to play for teams in the fledgling pro conferences. Had the Yellow Jackets not had such an impressive season, they would have been by-passed, this game would not have taken place, and next week Hegewisch would have played the Payne Boosters. Most who followed the powerhouses like the Kamm Brewers of South Bend, Chicago Gunners, Gillies Stars, or the all black American Giants gave little hope that the Yellow Jackets would win, or even play competitively against a powerhouse like Hegewisch. Nonetheless, the game was scheduled and would be played at Turner field on December 1st of 1935 in front of nearly 4,000 fans who had come from areas of Chicago and downstate Illinois, northwest Indiana, and beyond. The Hammond Times sports section on December 2, 1935, headlined their coverage "JACKETS SMACK HEGEWISCH; GET ANOTHER GAME," and reported in admirable terms,

" Maywood's building Yellow Jackets yesterday added to their long winning streak—the team is unbeaten in the last two seasons—by humbling Hegewisch A.C. 13 to 0 at Turner Field. Superior class and all-around power gave the Yellow Jackets a victory that might well have been more decisive. By virtue of their victory, the Jackets, who are champions of the Calumet Amateur Grid League, won the right to play next Sunday against Payne's Boosters in the charity contest which will conclude the football season."

The little giant from East Hammond called the Yellow Jackets was being noticed and talked about in broader circles of competition.

Newspapers and a Johnny Long Challenge

Other than the game played on September the 11th in East Chicago between the Chicago Bears and the Gillies Calumet All Stars, the most important and highly publicized game of the year would be the game played at Hammond's Turner Field on Sunday, December the 8th between the very powerful and successful Payne Dodgers Boosters and the Hammond Yellow Jackets. The Yellow Jackets were actually a replacement for the Gillies all Stars who did not do well in November, losing first to the Chicago Gunners 16 to 0 and then going on to play the all black American Giants and managing only a 6 to 6 tie game. (In actuality, tying the American Giants was a feat not properly acknowledged, for many high profile teams of that day refused to play the

Giants, understanding their speed and power and fearing a loss to them.)

Had the Gillies All Stars not tripped in November by losing one game and tying another, they would have been the team to play the Payne Boosters on December 8th and they would have been considered the underdog. The Payne Boosters were coming off of their finest football season, having gone undefeated in the Midwest U.S. Professional Football League and allowing only one touchdown to be scored upon them during the entire season. Their team was dripping with proven talent as reported in an article from the Hammond times, dated December 6, 1935:

"Tom Scully----quarterback of Chicago in 1933 and Ray Sloan, slipperiest runner seen in Chicago prairie football in a decade, lead the Payne Boosters into action. These two lads have started on the unbeaten Booster eleven which leads the Midwest League and which has allowed the opposition only one touchdown during the 1935 season.

The rest of the booster lineup includes lads who rated all-star teams in Chicago, and who later accomplished things on college elevens. Julius Szabo—190 pound fullback and Bronco Nagurski of the Midwest League, and Steve Milasevich, South Dakota star of 1930 are just a few of the booster starters."

It was Saturday, December 7th, and the Yellow Jackets were gathering for a 4:00 p.m. team meeting at Wusic's. Four guys were sitting on and around the red table near the chalkboard wall, reading the sports page from Friday. One of them, Pete Mindok yelled out to Fatty, "Hey, Fatty, have you seen this paper. Shit, these guys might as well be the Chicago Bears. Damn! Szabo, Nagurski, Milasevich. How about before the game you and Walt arrange for us to get their autographs? My kid brother would really like that."
Lots of laughter in the Yellow Jacket room.

Fatty responded, "I told you guys weeks ago not to read that shit. It isn't good for ya."

Guys kept coming into the room, several more with newspapers. Fatty, Walt, and Lefty just looked at each other, shook their heads and said nothing. Then as the room was nearly full with Yellow Jackets, all eyes focused on a figure in the doorway. It was Johnny Long. Johnny was the revered boxing coach of East Hammond who had fought professionally in Chicago, Detroit, and

New York. He was a conditioning fanatic for those he trained and for himself. If you were up at 5:00 a.m., you could see him running along the tracks each morning. He worked at the ice house on the southwest corner of East Hammond loading box cars all day, and he worked out regularly at the hub of boxing activity for Lake County, the Gary YMCA gym. He was the sparing partner for Tony Zale. Zale would become the country's middle Weight Champ and would have a series of fights with Rocky Graziano of New York that would for the entire history of boxing be considered classic.

The room became quiet except for several "Hi, Johnny" from various members of the team.

Johnny nodded appropriately then stated, "Lefty, Fatty, and Walt asked me to come over to talk to you guys today. So I said OK. If you don't mind, I'd like to tell you a story I'm not sure even Walt has heard. I was in new York about nine years ago, fighting one of my first ten-rounders, and I was scared. The guy I was fighting was a very skilled young fighter who had two years earlier won the New York Middle Weight Open Division of the Golden Gloves. He had seven professional fights since then, winning six with knockouts by the third round. I was his eighth fight. I knew that he was a smoother, more polished fighter than me, but I didn't think he was as conditioned as I was."

There was understood laughter from the room.

Johnny added humorously. "You think I'm a fanatic now about conditioning, you should have seen me then. Anyway, let's get back to the story. I had on my side two things that I thought were in my favor, and that convinced me that I could win. First was my conditioning. If he was gonna beat me, he'd have to knock me out, because if he didn't, he was gonna have to fight me hard for ten rounds. Second, I wanted that fight. I wanted it bad. I wanted to win. He was the home town boy and the odds makers couldn't even remember my name. I was some hick from some little town out west, and he was just doin' me a favor by letting me into a big fight. Well, we fought ten hard rounds, and I knew I was carrying him the last two because he was hangin' all over me, his legs were gone and he kept wrappin' me up. In the end, it was a split decision, and they gave it to him. But when we shook hands after, in the middle of the ring, he grabbed the back of my head with his gloved right hand, then leaned over to my ear and said, "Ya beat me. Great fight." I'll always remember that cause he was right, and he was a big man to say it to me.

Most of ya know that Walt is training with me even now during this football season for the Golden Gloves in February, and I'll tell you right now why he's goin' to win. Two reasons: First, Walt and I are goin' to make sure that he's in better condition than anybody he fights, and second," then Johnny paused and then said, "Well, you know the second because you know Walt."

Finally, he said, "I'm not sure that I've ever known a football team as conditioned as you guys are, and I've known a lot of teams." He paused again, then said, "So number one you've got. You will have to make up your minds about number two by yourselves. That's the way it always is. That's the way it was for me. That the way it's been for Walt." He nodded his head, paused again and said, "I'll be in the stands Sunday with the rest of most of East Hammond. See ya then." He then turned and left.

No one else left, and no one said anything. No one left for a very long time. When they finally did leave, they were a very sober team. They weren't yet ready for the game. But they would be tomorrow. Incidentally, Wolf won the heavy weight division of the Golden Gloves, knocking out each of his last two opponents in the second round.

That afternoon additional newspaper articles came out in the sports section of the Hammond Times:

"Headed by the Golarz brothers, 'Lefty' and 'Wolf,' the Maywood Champions will probably start as follows:

Ends—Milobar and G. Stoming

Tackles—Budnyk and Pulkowski

Guards—Gorski and Fyda

Center—Malakovich or Borbely

Halfbacks—W. and J. Golarz

Quarterback—Jasinski

Fullback—Novalik

Frank Thomas, Coach of Alabama's Rose Bowl Champions, may attend the game in order to inspect four or five of the players who plan on college careers. The Golarz brothers, Walt and John of the Yellow Jackets, are two of these lads meriting consideration."

The Yellow Jackets, however, were no longer thinking about newspaper articles. They had resolved to meet Johnny Long's challenge. They had made up their minds about number two. They wanted this game. They wanted it bad. And they had, to themselves, committed that tomorrow they were not going to play a game that they would lose.

Lefty and Walt
1935

A Field of Honor and Courage

Game day, Sunday, December 8th was a cold day. It was overcast and around 25 degrees. It was predicted that there would be light snow as the day progressed. The Yellow Jackets had all boarded the truck by 12:00 noon and were on their way to Turner Field. Kick off today would be 1:30 p.m. As they drove north, along Calumet Ave. toward the field, they were cheered and waved to by fans walking on both the east and west sides of Calumet making their way to the field. When they finally did get within range of the field, they found police officers directing and controlling traffic. Their truck was spotted and recognized, and police held traffic, giving them a clear path to the field area. They were directed to park, then got off the truck into the throngs of happy fans trying to get their attention. Fatty and Wusic led the team to the field and their bench on the home side. In the stands behind them were special seating sections for dignitaries such as the mayor, bankers, Chamber of Commerce members, representatives of the Knightstown Children's home and representatives from the tobacco fund for the War Veterans at Hines Hospital. The game was a charity game, so funds from donations and ticket sales were earmarked. Shortly after they got to their bench, the Payne Boosters ran onto the field and to the other side where their bench was located. They must have had 40 uniformed players and with them four or five coaches, all well dressed with heavy top coats and appropriate hats. There was, in addition, a complement of equipment people. The uniforms of the Boosters were new. Walt, sensing his team's discomfort, yelled out so all could hear, "They can only play 11 guys at a time, just like us." They started to laugh and began their warm ups. It was starting to snow a little harder.

For the coin-toss, the team sent out Walt and Pulkowski. The Payne Boosters won the toss and elected to receive. Walt kicked off. The kick was outstanding—very high and seeming to float beyond the end zone. The Boosters had to take the ball on the 20 yard line. On the very first play from scrimmage, their quarterback Scully dropped back about four yards very quickly and threw it to Sloan who had sped out of the backfield. Sloan caught it over his shoulder on the 30 yard line. Lefty caught him and tackled him on the 33. The game was underway.

On the next play Scully dropped back and then pitched it to their big fullback Julius Szabo as he came up the middle for seven yards where Walt brought him down. Walt then called a time out. Fatty came out with Mike Wusic. Everyone gathered around Walt. Fatty asked, "Do we need some different guys out here?"

Walt replied, "No, Fatty, there isn't anyone out here who isn't the right guy. We just need to break for a moment, clear our heads and get pissed off. We're ready now. They've shown us who they are. Now we're gonna show 'em who we are.

It was first and ten for the Boosters on the 40 yard line. They had moved 20 yards in two plays. The teams lined up. Scully barked out his signals. He snapped the ball, turned and dropped back four yards, as he planted his foot and turned back to pass, he was slammed to the ground by Pulkowski and Fyda. Pulkowski and Fyda then stood over him, and Pulkowski gave him a hand.

As he took his hand and got to his feet, Pulkowski said, "The name's Pulkowski. You're gonna see a lot of us this afternoon. Fyda chimed in, "It's Fyda with a "y.""

Pulkowski's remark that afternoon was right on. If it wasn't Pulkowski or Fyda, it was Malakovich, Stoming, Dotlich, Budnyk, or Borbely. The Yellow Jacket defense that had not allowed a touchdown all season was humming. But so was the defense of the Boosters. Lefty was getting tired just punting.

And then it happened, just before half time. Lefty's punting had put the Boosters in a box. They had the ball first and ten on their own 25. The teams lined up. Pulkowski and Borbely licked their chops. Then Scully dropped back and barked signals. The ball was snapped. It came right back to him, and before the Yellow Jacket defensive line could close, Scully pitched to Sloan who sped towards the side line and the line of scrimmage. Three yards before he got to the line of scrimmage, he stopped quickly, set and let a pass fly 40 yards to Julius Szabo who was now running full speed to the Yellow Jacket end zone, having passed by all Yellow Jacket defenders whom he had caught off guard. The score was Boosters 6, Yellow Jackets 0. The conversion attempt was missed.

It was half time, and the light snow that had been predicted had turned into a wet and heavy lake effect snow with some wind. There was already nearly an inch and a half on the ground, and the snow was now coming about an inch an hour. Further, it was getting difficult to see through it.

In their half time huddle, Fatty and Walt felt that there was no fear on the part of their team, no sense of awe for their opponent, no lack of confidence, but rather a resolve to go back and win. The stern stuff that was rekindled by Johnny Long was still there. It was still there, and everyone in that huddle knew it. They knew they would not let loose of it. They were here to play a game that they would not lose.

Walt then stood up in the huddle, looked at his team, and said, "Rotate, rotate, rotate.

We've met them and their famous names mean nothing. They're just 11 guys who are getting tired. So, we rotate, rotate, and rotate, and we wear 'em down. You'll know we have 'em when between plays they go to one knee with a hand on the ground, their chests heaving, struggling for a breath of air. When that happens, and it will, we take this game away cause it's ours. Let's go play football."

The Yellow Jackets came back to the field looking and feeling sharp, alert, clear-headed, and quick. And, they were getting the ball. The Boosters kicked off. A great kick, so the Yellow Jackets started on the 20 yard line. Then it began as it had in so many games this season. Walt, five yards off tackle; Lefty, three yards up the middle; Novalik, four yards up the middle; Lefty, four yards off tackle. They were chipping away at a block of granite called the Booster defense that had allowed only one touchdown this season against the best teams in the Midwest Conference. Chipping away at a block of granite, but chipping with diamond bits. Enock, four yards; Lefty, four yards; Enoch, three yards; Joe Golec, six yards. Chipping away and watching cracks beginning to show. Lefty two yards; Golec, four yards. A Booster lineman with his knee on the ground. Walt, three yards; Novalik, four yards; Golec, three yards. Two Booster linemen. Novalik, six yards; Lefty, seven yards, and, finally, Walt up the middle, through the line, through their secondary and into the end zone. The Yellow Jackets had broken through, and the Booster defense was tired. The conversion was missed, and the score was Yellow Jackets 6, Boosters 6. The drive had taken most of the third quarter, and it was snowing heavily.

The remainder of the third quarter, and the first half of the final quarter was a dogfight in the middle of the field with neither team able to really move the ball. Then, with four minutes remaining, the Yellow Jackets got the ball on their own 40 yard line. And it began again: Walt, four yards up the middle; Walt, six yards off tackle; Novalik, five yards; Lefty, four yards; Golec, four yards; Enoch, four yards; Walt, five yards; Lefty... Novalik.... At that point, no Booster lineman was standing between plays and the exhaled breath from their deep-breathing could be seen as a small cloud just above the snowy cold ground on which they were placing their very cold hands to rest themselves.

The Yellow Jackets looked at them from their huddle as they prepared to call and run their next play. And then the whistle blew as the refs declared that time had run out. But those on the field that day knew that the whistle was only marking what had already happened. The end of the game had preceded that whistle. The Yellow Jackets knew it and so did the Boosters. The Yellow Jackets had played a powerful and honorable opponent, and they had not lost. And they would always remember that. As would the Payne Boosters and anyone else who understood sport.

Johnny Long stood in the stands that day long after the game was over. He stood there with his hands in his pockets and watched it snow. He stood there until he could hardly see the field except in his mind. A vision of a field of honor and courage that he would always have to treasure. A field of honor and courage where the children of immigrants, though hungry and ill-equipped, demonstrated to everyone and, most importantly, to themselves their worth and value in football and in the challenges and opportunities that life would ask of them and provide to them. So, he just stood there and watched it snow.

Independence Day

Getting to the 4:00 p.m. team meeting at Wusic's on Monday was a little tough. The light snow that started on Sunday turned into a full lake effect blizzard, and it snowed all night and didn't stop until early Monday morning. The Yellow Jackets still stiff and sore from Sunday's contest found themselves shoveling snow for their families and neighbors.

It was 10:00 a.m. Monday morning in the 1100 block of Moss Avenue when Kal said to Lefty, "Nothing like a little morning workout to limber up the old muscles, eh Left?"

"Just keep shovelin,' Kal. Ma said she would have some coffee for us when we got done."

"Where's Walt, Left?"

"He took off early with Fyda and Milobar to do Wusic's gas station, said he'd meet us there later."

"Y' know, Left, as you look down Moss here towards the coal yard, it's really pretty...y' know, like a winter wonderland."

"I'll give ya "wonderland" Just keep shovelin'."

"Lefty, you have no romance in your heart, except maybe when you're thinkin' of Gigs.

Lefty stopped shoveling, leaned on his shovel, stared down the street at the snow in the direction of Helen's house and just said, "Yeah."

Eventually the two buddies got back to work, finished and went in for that cup of coffee.

At 4:00 p.m. the team assembled at Wusic's for their last team meeting of the season. Fatty started things off. "First thing, old man Wusic thanks you guys for comin' this morning to dig out the station. He really appreciated that. Second, for you coffee lovers like Lefty and Kal back there, that aroma you're smelling is fresh brewed coffee. It's a gift from the Polish National Alliance here in East Hammond. Mr. Gajewski and Mr. Wleklinski brought it over this morning. There's probably enough, if you're careful, to last the winter. You guys collecting coal might even get a full cup after your night hunts on the tracks. Just remember when you see 'em in church or wherever, thank 'em for the coffee. They'll really like that. Now, I need to turn it over to Walt. He wants to talk about whether or not you want to continue in the league next year."

Walt began, "Well guys, we need to decide…"

"Walt, excuse me, but can I interrupt," said Heinie Milobar.

"Sure, Heinie, what you got?"

"Well, before you get started, a lot of us guys have been talkin', and we know a lot of what's been goin' on. We know that you and Fatty and a few others have had a lot of meetings to go to at the Mayor's office and the Chamber of Commerce, and we know they got pissed off when we did our own special collection for the Kopinski family at the homecoming game. And, we know that there's no promises that we'll have more home games next year and that they may be at Turner Field, and that they don't want us takin' on our own games like we did Crown Point this year unless they approve it. So, we been talkin' and we're feelin' like it ain't our team anymore and we don't like it." Heinie stopped, and there was a lot of quiet talk, some "yeahs," and a great deal of nods affirming support of Heinie's remarks.

Walt looked at the team then said, "Unless I'm misreading this, and I don't think I am, you guys look like you're ready for a vote. Is that right?" Lots of "yeahs" and nods of support and approval. Then Walt said, "Fatty, Wusic stay in here. Want you in on this vote too. OK, anybody in favor of staying in the league raise your hand."

No hands went up. Walt continued to wait and still no hands. He looked around the room. Still no hands.

"OK, how many of you guys want out of the league and back on our own?"

Immediately every hand in the room went up. Then Walt raised his hand. "Guess we're out of the league."

Applause and cheers in the room. Then Walt continued, "Lefty, Fatty, Gorski, would you guys go with me tomorrow to City Hall? I think we should tell 'em right away." Nods of agreement from Lefty and the others.

Then Walt said, "Fatty had had a few items."

"Thanks, Walt. Some of you guys have an old shirt or jersey layin' around here. Please take 'em home with you today. Would a few of you guys stay after and help Wusic wrap the tarps real good for the winter then put 'em away up where Mike keeps 'em? Finally, those of you guys goin' out tonight to collect coal, if you come here afterwords, have some coffee. Mike will show you where it's gonna be kept. That's all I got. Anybody else?"

No one had anything. The meeting was over, but leaving today was hard, so a second pot of coffee was brewed and another couple of small logs went into the pot-bellied stove. Lots of just small talk, not a lot about football, but it wasn't because they weren't thinkin' about it. Just didn't feel like talkin' about it right now. It had been a great season and no one really wanted it to end. Oh, there would be next year's season, but that would be next year. So, the small talk continued and the coffee got sipped slowly, very slowly.

In Hard Times and Good

After the winter storm of December 8th and 9th, there was little additional snowfall. However it stayed cold, often in the teens. The cold snap provoked a second run on coal at the tracks, and that coal was now nearly gone. Buying a half ton of coal was so expensive for families focused upon food. And when it was bought, poverty forced the purchase of the lowest grade of coal which didn't heat as well and which left an incombustible residue fused into large, irregular lumps known as clinkers. If residents of East Hammond were not careful as they shook their furnace grates to remove ash and allow the fire in the furnace to breathe, the clinkers could get stuck between the grates. Forcing them loose could break a grate. This would then require the purchase of a new grate, shutting the furnace down to allow it to cool, then replacing the grate. This was expensive and, in addition, it would be cold in the house for an extended period which, of course, might cause a water pipe to freeze. Such were the daily concerns and plights of the poor. Poverty was never fun and fond memories rarely resulted from it.

Nonetheless, as Christmas neared, hearts in East Hammond turned to the joys of the activities surrounding that blessed event. On December 23rd in the early morning, Lefty and Walt went for a Christmas tree from Mike Wusic's truck. They were early enough so they did not get stuck with the last of the trees. The one they selected actually had some shape and did not need to be forced through the front door. Ma did not lose her purse this year and had been saving twenty cents a week since October so that she could have a proper Wigilia meal. Pa loved his pierogi so there would be more than an ample supply of those this year. Ma's brother and sister-the-law, the Kots, would again be coming with their two children. But this year they would be bringing the fish dishes, including the herring in oil. This would allow Ma and Kate to focus more on some other dishes like the homemade breads, kapusta, (sauerkraut), and homemade soups. Kal and Alex Fyda had been invited by Walt and Lefty and had been advised to simply bring themselves.

Finally the 24th of December came and with it the promise of the first substantial snow since the heavy snow of early December. It was expected to start at midday and snow into and through the night. Kate had earlier in the day decorated the tree with Anne and Andy, and as was her custom, she bought them each a new ornament for the tree. Ma's Wigilia dinner brought delight. All the traditional foods were there, plus more than sufficient pierogi with all the expected fillings: cheese, kapusta, and potato. The Kots came with more than enough to feed the hosts that Christ had for the Sermon on the Mount. There would be fish for Wigilia, Christmas Day and the Feast of St. Stephen on the 26th, and then some.

After dinner, Pa pulled out his treasured Polish Christmas song book. They sat that night after dinner, and with this book as their guide, along with their own knowledge of their favorite songs, they sang. They sang *Dzisiaj w Bethejem* (*This Day in Bethlehem*); they sang *Bog Sie Rodzi* (*God is Born*); they sang *Lulajze, Jezuniu* (*Lullaby, Sweet Jesus*). Then they sang, and they sang some more, and when Pa judged that they had sung enough, he closed his book, and they had the children open their few gifts, purchased from carefully saved pennies and nickels.

The walk to Midnight Mass at St. Mary's Church was a snowy one that night, but it was a light snow, and although some several inches had already fallen, it was not hard to walk through. So, the small but happy band of Lefty, Walt, Kate, Kal, and Alex walked. They sang as they walked, the Christmas songs still resonating in their hearts. They did not sing quietly, for Lefty loved to sing, a gift that would be inherited by his daughter Barbara. They walked down Moss Avenue to Tapper where they turned right and went to Ames Avenue. There Kate, Walt, and Alex waited while Kal went for Mary Bindas, one house away and while Lefty went to Helen Grelak's house, three doors down. Soon they were again on their way, now a slightly larger band. As they walked on this snowy Christmas Eve, they talked, they laughed, they sang some more and they enjoyed each other's company. They had just had their Wigilia and they weren't hungry.

It was a time now to take a moment and give thanks. So, they continued to walk, now past Conkey and just several more blocks where St.

Mary's stood on the corner of Morris and Tapper. As they approached that night, individuals as well as other small groups were arriving, coming from everywhere, but mostly from East Hammond. The church tonight would be full, and by the time Christmas Eve Mass began, many would be standing in the back for want of a seat. The nuns had the responsibility of cleaning and of decorating the church. But there were not the number, nor the ornate decorations we find today. There were just not enough funds. So, the decorations were simple. There were nativity figures arranged in a traditional mode on the St. Joseph's altar, and the main altar had two flowers, one right and one left of the tabernacle at the altar's center.

For the mass itself, there were six altar boys, dressed in black cassocks and white serplices. One of the altar boys in the last pair carried the senser thurible and boat containing incense which would be lit later during the mass to accompany the priest's special blessing of the congregation.

Altars
Old Saint Mary's Church

Fr. Szczukowski was the primary focal point of the entire celebration of the mass and as Christmas was a major church celebration, all that he wore that night signified the joy and importance of the occasion. From his alb to his maniple and stole, and finally to his outer garment, the chasuble, all was white with touches of gold. If it was intended that he also have the look of royalty, he did.

Walt motioned to Lefty. He, Alex and Kate had found seats near the St. Joseph's altar. There was not quite enough room, but if they squeezed in, they could make it. The church was filling rapidly now. The hour was near and the tower bells were announcing the imminent beginning of the mass. When the bells stopped, everyone knew the mass was about to begin. Soon thereafter, the little tinkling bell, fashioned on the door frame of the entrance to the sacristy would be gently struck by the lead altar boy. The bell announced that the little procession of three pairs of altar boys and the priest were now coming out of the sacristy. The mass was beginning. The congregation stood and the choir and entire congregation began to sing the traditional beginning of St. Mary's Christmas Mass song, *Wsrod Mocnej Ciszy*: "Angels from Heaven *sang, waking the shepherds. Rise, greet the newborn son of David, King Emanuel."*

Lefty removed his overcoat, exposing his Yellow Jacket sweater, white shirt and tie, crowned by the navy blue and yellow plaid Christmas scarf that matched so appropriately the color of his sweater and the navy blue border around his Yellow Jacket emblem. Helen had given it to him on the walk to church. She gently touched his sleeve and motioned for him to remove it in church, but he just smiled at her and kept it on.. Then he held her hand. Lefty glanced at Walt and felt badly that he had no one with him tonight, but then Walt was okay. Tomorrow, Christmas Day, he was going to have dinner with the family of a young lady named Sylvia that he really liked in Calumet City. As Lefty then glanced toward the center aisle of church, he noticed Mr. Kopinski in his wheel chair. Next to him in the pew was his wife and next to her Walter Kwolek. Walter turned his head, spotted Lefty and smiled. Lefty winked.

Then Lefty just looked up at the altar. And he thought of himself and his Yellow Jackets. None was alcoholic, no one had committed suicide. No one was in jail, no one had been shot or killed. Behind him in the choir Sarah Kopinski was singing with the other eighth graders, and next to Lefty in their filled community church was the woman he was sure he would marry. He had just eaten his mother's Wigilia meal and sung from his father's treasured song book. Tonight was truly a night to give thanks and not be afraid to feel the joy. Tomorrow he would shovel snow, and tomorrow night and the night after he would collect coal on the tracks. And by next week he would again be hungry, but despite that hunger and want, he would have the pleasure of nurturing half cups of coffee with his Yellow Jacket comrades at Wusic's. And he would know that even though they had not the resources to fill those cups, they did not need to. For in the real things, they knew their cups "runneth over."

Epilogue

In 2009 I wrote and published *When The Yellow jackets Played*. This book was based almost exclusively on stories reported to me by my father "Lefty" over the years. The book also relied upon information from the memory of my Aunt Rose, several pages of notes taken by my cousin Tony after conversations with Lefty, and my own memory. The entire content of the book focused on the 1936 football season—the last season played by the Yellow Jackets.

The content of this book, *Yellow Jacket Football in Hard Times and Good*, begins in the fall of 1934 and ends on Christmas Eve of 1935. Thus, the content of this book contains stories from the 1934 season, and the entire 1935 football season. The book contains stories that go beyond football. Stories that reveal the daily lives of these Yellow Jackets and their ethnic community as they struggled to deal with the challenges of life in a community so hard hit by the great depression. The contents of this book came again from stories reported to me by my father, by more of the memories of my Aunt Rose, and from my own knowledge of the community and neighborhood in which I was born and spent my early years.

In addition, much of the information comes from a plethora of newspaper articles from 1934 through 1939. Researching for these articles took hundreds of hours. When the book in 2009 was published, my intent was primarily to preserve the stories Lefty had shared with so much excitement. However, the response to this little book was so overwhelmingly positive and filled with responses that conveyed a feeling of disappointment at it being so short, that I decided to explore the possibility of extending this saga.

At the time of the writing *When the Yellow Jackets Played*, neither I nor my family was aware that the articles eventually found were even in existence. To locate them was actually quite laborious, but once the first was found, an actual report of the 1935 Yellow Jacket vs. Crown Point game, the need to continue searching for more was compelling. In the end, some 28 articles were found, many specific to the Yellow Jackets and some adjunct but related to their play.

There will be a third book published, probably in 2011. That book will take the reader from 1937 through 1949. This last book will focus on the East Hammond Community's crawl out of the depression and upon life during the years of World War II, and into the late forties. The sources will again come from stories reported to me by Lefty and my Aunt Rose and others. This time, however, I will be able to relate my own vivid memories of those years as I spent the majority of my time in that neighborhood with my parents and my Busia, even attending grade school at St. Mary's.

Many characters from the first two books will still grace the pages of this third book and, of course, there will be stories, stories, and more stories. If Lefty taught me one thing, he taught me that we all love good stories and the stories of book three will be good stories.

After football Walt and Lefty pursued other avenues of interest and accomplishments, and their many children and grandchildren also inherited their admiration for education and learning and have enjoyed a wide variety of pursuits in medicine, business, sales, construction, acting, music, journalism, writing, education, finance and banking.

So, did football continue to be important in the Golarz and Yellow Jacket family? Yes. But what is hoped, is that what also continued was an understanding that a rich life is so much more than success at football, or any sport, or any profession. That is what we believe Lefty understood in St. Mary's church at Midnight Mass on that snowy night in December of 1935. Something that he, Walt, and so many of the Yellow Jackets hoped that they conveyed to their friends, families, and the neighborhood from which they came. And they would tell you, if they could, that if this is the message that you took away from this story of the Yellow Jackets, then it was for them a good, clean, hard-fought and worthy game. And they would pour you a half cup of coffee and smile.

About the Cover

All of the items on the cover of this book are either the actual and authentic items that were referred to in the book or were purchased to best represent an item of the book.

In the upper left-hand corner of the picture is the actual Yellow Jacket sweater of Lefty Golarz. We know of no other team sweater in existence. The "YJ" letters on the sweater also belonged to Lefty.

After the publication of my first Yellow Jacket book, *When the Yellow Jackets Played*, we received from Buddy Borbely the emblem "Yellow Jacket 35" shown in the picture on the pocket of Lefty's sweater. The emblem belonged to Buddy's father, Kal Borbely, Yellow Jacket center and Lefty's life-long friend.

The large chest in which most of the items are placed was the same ocean-crossing chest brought to America around 1907 by Walt and Lefty's mother or father.

The round sandstone grinding wheel in the lower left-hand corner of the picture is—yes, you guessed it—the grinding wheel made by Walt and Lefty in 1932 or 1933. It has stood the test of time and may soon again be fashioned with an appropriate mechanism so that it can do again its intended work.

The football. Ah, the football. Given to the author by Lefty around 1947 from way back in Lefty's bedroom closet. Dusted off and "Here's an old football for ya, kid. Used to be mine." Yellow Jacket football??

The boxing gloves—two pair of these. Belonged to Lefty and Walt. Given to the author by Lefty around 1947 or 1948. Lots of backyard and garage boxing done with these.

Just below the boxing gloves, the trophy given to Lefty from the nuns of St. Mary's School. Inscribed on the cup are the words "Honor Student; S.M.S.; Class of 1930," as reported in *When the Yellow Jackets Played*.

The chair front right is a "telephone chair" from the house of Lefty and Helen. Vintage unknown but quite old.

The Christmas bulbs represent the kind of ornament that would have been used at this time to decorate a family Christmas tree. These were purchased by my wife Marion at an antique store in Bloomington, Indiana. Vintage 1930's or so.

The lantern in the picture belonged to Lefty and was part of his collected tools, many from his father Joseph Golarz. Used on nights to collect coal?

On the seat of the chair, a little change purse, probably much like the change purse lost somewhere on the train tracks that cold and windy December night in 1934, by Mary Golarz, the mother of Walt and Lefty. A purse never found. Replaced for this picture by one found in an antique store by Marion Golarz.

After long searching, a coffee pot of the 1930 era. Can you see it heating on the small wood burning stove in the Yellow Jacket room at Wusic's, or possibly in Ma Golarz's for the enjoyment of some Yellow Jackets. You can smell the coffee as it percolates and fills the air with that fresh-made aroma that will soon be poured into the waiting cups of some grateful young men.

Finally, in the most upper-left-hand corner of the picture the navy blue plaid scarf that so elegantly matched both Lefty's Yellow Jacket sweater upon which it is laid and the navy blue trim around the "YJ" letters. Lefty remained fond of plaids all of his life and fonder still of the young girl who in the story placed it there. It and they matched so well all the rest of their lives.

Hope you enjoy our picture as much as we enjoyed creating it for you.

Ray and Marion Golarz

About the Author

Raymond J. Golarz was born in 1940 in East Hammond, Indiana, the setting for this book. He spent his earliest formative years in this community, even attending much of his elementary school years at St. Mary's school. As a young adult, he spent his early working years employed in steel production, processing, and forging plants. He married Marion Joyce Simpson and together they have six children: Tanya, Michael, Scott, Jocelyn, Daniel and Thomas John. He became a teacher and later directed delinquency prevention programs near Chicago. For years he taught law enforcement officers before becoming an assistant superintendent and superintendent of schools. He taught psychology at St. Joseph's College, Purdue Calumet, and City College in Seattle. He has keynoted major conferences in every large province in Canada and in virtually every state in the United States. He is the co-author of *Restructuring Schools for Excellence Through Teacher Empowerment* published in 1991, co-author with his wife Marion of *The Power of Participation* published in 1995 and the author of *When the Yellow Jackets Played* published in 2009.

He received his doctorate from Indiana University in 1980. He currently resides in Bloomington, Indiana, with his wife Marion.

His personal "Rosebud" continues to be the 1930s and 1940s neighborhood of East Hammond.

His email is <u>mgolarz@hotmail.com</u>